*An
entertaining
authoritative
handbook
for everyone
who takes
pictures*

How to make GOOD

PICTURES

*by the
editors of
Eastman
Kodak
Company*

Contents

INTRODUCTION

31st Edition, First 1965 Printing
Printed in the United States of America

This isn't a book about cameras, per se. If you're one of those who regard them with the same passion others lavish on hi-fi components or Model T Fords, you'll suffer no scarcity of volumes that probe and praise their mechanical wonders. But in this book, cameras are regarded strictly as a means to an end and that end is pictures, the kind of pictures most people snap—pictures of their children and family, of the places they visit, and of the things they do.

It isn't an especially technical kind of book, because, for most of us, technicalities and fun don't necessarily mix. It simply points out some of the features which make good pictures superior to run-of-the-mill pictures and suggests ideas for shooting good pictures with the least possible fuss and expense.

The type of pictures it explores are snapshots—all kinds of snapshots of many different subjects. Is there a baby in the house? We have a whole section devoted to "Snapshots of Babies." As baby grows, you'll want to refer to the section on "Snapshots of Children." Another section will show you how to take the best snapshots of Mom and Dad, and other grown-ups. The section on flowers will help you to enjoy your garden year-round in your pictures. Going on a trip? The section on "Vacation and Travel" will help you to make the most of your picturetaking opportunities. Do you have a pet? Like sports? Or, is scenery your camera's prime target? This book contains helpful hints on taking better snapshots of all these things.

We also talk about taking snapshots indoors with flash, photoflood, or existing light. In case you're one of the people who likes to know about the technical side of things, we included several sections for you toward the end of the book. One is on how color films work and another is on the technical workings of photography.

And of all snapshot ideas, here is the one that will be most valuable in providing you with a reputation as an expert photographer. Nobody's pictures are all good. Even the most practiced professional turns out some poor pictures. He just doesn't show them to anybody.

MAKING SHARP SNAPSHOTS

Loading your camera

Loading film incorrectly is like pumping gasoline into the radiator of a car rather than its fuel tank. Nothing much starts unless this initial chore is handled properly.

Camera instruction booklets almost always contain a step-by-step resume of correct loading methods. Trying a couple of practice runs with a new camera is always an excellent idea before starting with the real thing.

Correct loading is crucial because the same reaction of film and light that makes a picture inside your camera can make a picture-spoiling blob if allowed to occur during loading operations. This is why loading in bright sunlight is a chancy maneuver. If trapped in Death Valley, the Gobi Desert, or some other location where direct sunlight is inescapable, load in the shadow of your body.

Roll film consists of a length of opaque colored paper with a shorter length of film fastened inside it. The paper not only protects the film but provides the indispensable picture numbers. On Kodak roll film, each number is preceded and followed by the name of the film as a reminder against using camera settings or flash distances for a different kind of film than you actually have.

7

Film for 35mm cameras has no backing paper; it is protected from light by the metal magazine in which it is packaged. After loading and closing the camera, advance the film two or three times to move any possibly exposed area out of the way. Be sure to set the film counter, or you'll have no record of how many pictures you've snapped. Before opening the camera back, you must roll the entire roll of film back into its metal magazine. Your camera manual will tell you the correct way to do this.

The newest development in film loading is the Kodak Instamatic Camera with the Kodapak Cartridge. The film is enclosed in a molded lighttight cartridge, which can be easily dropped into and removed from, the camera even in direct sunshine. Through a window on the camera back, the name of the film, the picture number, and the total number of pictures available are visible.

Film

Film comes in many sizes for different kinds of cameras, and in many types for different kinds of pictures. Film is a light-sensitive material, so protect it from unwanted light by loading and unloading your camera in subdued light.

Finish up the roll within a few weeks and take it to your photo dealer for processing. You can have your color film processed by a Kodak laboratory or another processing laboratory.

BLACK-AND-WHITE PRINTS	For black-and-white prints, use Kodak Verichrome Pan Film with daylight and flash or Kodak Plus-X Pan Film with daylight and flash in 35mm cameras.
COLOR PRINTS	For color prints, use Kodacolor-X Film with daylight and blue flash.
COLOR SLIDES	For color slides, use Kodachrome II Film for Daylight, Kodachrome-X Film, or Kodak Ektachrome-X Film with daylight or blue flash.

Refer to page 149 for more information on films.

Film instruction sheet

In packages of all Kodak films, except Kodak Verichrome Pan Film, there is an instruction sheet. This sheet tells you how to use the film to get the best possible pictures.

Data for Verichrome Pan Film is printed on the beginning of the backing paper that protects each roll.

Film instructions are important. Changes in films, flashbulbs, and camera equipment may alter the data in this book or other publications. But you can always consult the Film Instruction Sheet or the beginning of the backing paper for recommendations that will be up-to-date.

The first part of the instruction sheet tells you how to expose the film in daylight.

CX 135 Kodacolor-X FILM

FOR COLOR PRINTS AND ENLARGEMENTS

For taking pictures in DAYLIGHT or with BLUE FLASHBULBS

☀ DAYLIGHT PICTURES

FOR AUTOMATIC CAMERAS OR EXPOSURE METERS

The film speed is a measure of the film's sensitivity to light. Set the film speed dial on your camera or exposure meter at 64 to assure proper exposure of this film.

SETTING CAMERAS WITHOUT AN EXPOSURE METER

DAYLIGHT EXPOSURE TABLE FOR *KODACOLOR-X* FILM			
Set the *shutter speed at 1/125 second* and the lens at the f-number indicated under the lighting condition below that matches the lighting on your subject.			
Bright or Hazy Sun (Distinct Shadows)	Cloudy Bright (No Shadows)	Heavy Overcast	Open Shade†

f11*	f5.6	f4	f4

*f5.6 for backlighted closeup subjects—f16 for brilliant scenes, such as those containing much sand or snow.
†Subject shaded from sun but lighted by a large area of sky.

For ready reference, tape this table to your camera case.

Flash pictures

Taking flash pictures is made easy with the new-style instruction sheets. All you have to do is select the flash strip that matches the reflector and bulb you are using, then tape the strip to your equipment. Estimate the distance from your flash to your subject and find the lens opening (*f*-number) for that distance on the strip. Set your shutter speed at 1/30 second and use the indicated lens opening.

The second part of the instruction sheet contains the flash information (as below). You can cut out the flash strips from the film instruction sheet, or you can buy pregummed "Flash Stickers" from your photo dealer.

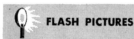

FLASH PICTURES

USE BLUE FLASHBULBS
(Clear bulbs are no longer recommended.)
Use blue flashbulbs and fresh batteries. Weak batteries cause flash failure. Choose a flash-exposure strip from the group below for your type of flash reflector and bulb. Set your shutter speed at **1/25, 1/30,** or **1/40** second. Estimate the distance in feet between *flash* and *subject*. Set your lens opening at the f-number in the block below this distance. You can cut out one of the strips below and tape it to your equipment. If your camera has flash guide numbers on the lens mount, set it at the guide number below for your flash reflector and bulb.

Guide Nos.	Reflector Types	Flash-bulbs	KODACOLOR-X Film 1/30 sec					
50		AG-1B	feet	4-5	6	8-10	12	15-20	25
			lens opening	11	8	5.6	4	2.8	2
65		AG-1B M2B	feet	4-5	6	8-10	12	15-20	25
			lens opening	16	11	8	5.6	4	2.8
100	*	AG-1B M2B	feet	5	6	8-10	12-15	20	25
			lens opening	22	16	11	8	5.6	4
95		M3B M5B 5B	feet	4-5	6	8-10	12	15-20	25
			lens opening	22	16	11	8	5.6	4
140	*	M3B M5B 5B	feet	6	8	10-12	15	20-25	
			lens opening	22	16	11	8	5.6	

*Polished bowl reflector.

If you want to use higher shutter speeds, and you are sure your camera will synchronize properly with the bulb concerned, do this: For any shutter speed up to 1/125 second use the f-number in the block to the right of the one you would normally use.

Cameras

All modern cameras can take pictures in black-and-white and in color, and the color pictures can be either slides or prints. Like cars, all cameras have the same basic parts, but some have more "power" and features than others. "Simple" cameras are restricted to use in sunlight or near-by pictures with flash.

Your interest in this book shows that you want wider picturetaking ability. So let's pinpoint your interest. Are you "content oriented" or "technique oriented"? This is market-research talk, which means—Do you just want pictures without fuss, or do camera settings fascinate you?

If you just want pictures, the Kodak Instamatic Cameras are for you. To load, just drop in a Kodapak Cartridge. The Instamatic 300 Camera and higher-numbered models adjust themselves to suit the light. An electric eye looks at the subject and tells the lens what to do. So you just aim the Instamatic 300 or 400 Camera and shoot. The Instamatic 500 and higher-numbered cameras require that you focus; that is, adjust for distance. You also set the shutter speed—but you can leave it at 1/250 second for most everything. These cameras can also cope with poorer daylight and greater flash distances.

The Instamatic 700 and 800 Cameras also have "automated" flash photography. When you focus, the lens sets itself for the right exposure. So the Instamatic Cameras come closest yet to George Eastman's "You press the button, we do the rest."

Other kinds of automatic cameras take a little more work on your part than the Instamatic Cameras. You must "tell" the light meter on such a camera the speed of the film in the camera. You do this by setting the film speed (or ASA speed) on the dial on your camera. The film speed is a number assigned to a film to tell a meter how much exposure that particular film will need. You'll find the film speed number on your film instruction sheet. After you set the film speed, aim the camera at the subject, and the camera will automatically set itself for the proper exposure. The only thing left for you to do is focus and snap the picture.

Unless your camera is the "fixed focus" type, it is always necessary to focus. If you have a fixed-focus lens, you can take pictures from 5 feet to infinity. All other lenses must be focused for the distance to your subject. You do this because a lens can't see sharply everything within its view, but it can be adjusted so that all objects over a certain range of distance will form sharp images. If you forget to focus, part or all of your picture will be fuzzy and unsharp.

Perhaps you have a roll-film or 35mm camera with strictly "do-it-yourself" settings. Or it may be one of the newer cameras with electric eyes that you can elect to use or not. In either case these cameras take more "doing"— they suit the "technique oriented" owner. They also have the widest picturetaking range.

These cameras have three settings that you must make— lens opening, shutter speed, and focusing. Lens openings, or f-numbers, are numbers that indicate the size of the opening that lets the light into the camera. The larger the number, the smaller the opening. A large number like $f11$ lets a small amount of light into the camera, while a small number like $f2.8$ means a larger opening and a lot of light striking the film.

The shutter speed determines the length of time that the light is striking the film. A shutter-speed marking of 125 means that light is hitting the film for $1/125$ second. A speed of $1/250$ second lets the light strike the film for half the time of $1/125$, and $1/60$ second lets the light in for twice as long as $1/125$. If the lighting conditions permit, use a shutter speed of $1/125$ or $1/250$ second. These higher shutter speeds help reduce the effect of camera movement, which is the most common cause of blurred pictures.

If you are using an exposure meter, find the film speed to set on your meter in the film instruction sheet. If you don't have an exposure meter, use the Daylight Exposure Table in your film instruction sheet. Find the box with the lighting condition that matches the lighting on your subject. Beneath it, the table will indicate which lens opening (*f*-number) to use. The table also tells you the correct shutter speed.

It is always necessary to focus an adjustable camera. As you know, focusing adjusts the lens so that all objects over a certain range of distance will form sharp images in your picture. Estimate the distance to your subject and set the focus on that number. Objects at the distance you focus on will always be sharp. Small lens openings, such as *f*11, give a wider range of sharpness before and behind your subject than do large lens openings, such as *f*4. The range of sharpness is always narrower at closeup distances than at those farther away. In all your closeup snapping, remember that there isn't much room for focusing error.

Cameras that adjust offer a selection of different shutter times. With Kodak Verichrome Pan Film, the basic outdoor setting is 1/125 second. This tends to reduce the effect of camera movement, since the camera budges only half as far in 1/125 as in 1/60. It doesn't, however, eliminate movement altogether, and whatever shutter time you employ, try to keep your camera as rock-steady as possible. The usual basic daylight setting for color films is 1/125 second.

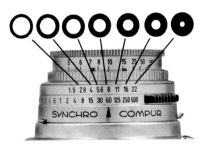

All the numbers on a camera's shutter scale are fractions of a second. For example, 30 is 1/30 second, 60 is 1/60 second. The higher the number, the shorter the shutter time, and the more useful it is for photographing fast action. The f-numbers indicate the size of the opening through which light can pass. The larger numbers represent the smaller lens openings.

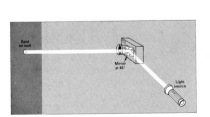

To test your camera-handling steadiness, fasten a pocket mirror over the lens with a rubber band, train a flashlight or slide projector on the mirror, and aim the camera so that you get a sharp reflection on a wall. Squeeze the shutter release as gently as you can. If the reflection jumps appreciably, keep practicing until you can hold it quite steady.

Exposures for adjustable cameras

Many adjustable cameras still require that you set the correct lens opening and shutter speed for best exposure. An exposure merely consists of a certain-size opening (ƒ-number) through which light can reach the film, plus the period of time (shutter time) that the opening is uncovered. When the beginning of the backing paper on a roll of Kodak Verichrome Pan Film recommends basic settings of 1/125 second at ƒ16 for pictures in bright sunlight, it merely establishes a home base for exposure.

For average subjects, use a shutter speed of 1/125 or 1/250 second if the lighting conditions permit. A higher shutter speed reduces the possibility of camera movement, which is the main cause of blurred pictures. Should your subject be a fast-moving one, it might be necessary to use a briefer shutter time, let's say 1/500 second, as insurance against blurring. Once you've cut the shutter time in half, though, the only way to assure that the same amount of light reaches the film is by shifting the lens opening so that twice as much light can pass through. This would call for a lens setting of ƒ8. Since 1/125 second at ƒ16 and 1/500 second at ƒ8 permit the same amount of light to enter the camera, they are equivalent exposures.

To make this business of selecting equivalent exposures a rather easy one, both the lens and shutter settings marked on most cameras are drawn up so that each is generally

Kodak Flash Stickers are pregummed stickers which can be applied directly to your camera equipment. They are direct reading, and give the lens opening to use for flash at different distances.

The Daylight Dial in the **Kodak Master Photoguide** gives the right lens and shutter settings for a variety of films and lighting conditions.

either double or half its immediate neighbor. Shutter times progress through 1/30, 1/60, 1/125, 1/250, or similar relationships. A lens opening of $f1.4$ lets in twice as much light as $f2$, which lets in twice as much as $f2.8$, and so on through $f4$, $f5.6$, $f8$, $f11$, $f16$, and $f22$. Some cameras have a widest lens opening of $f3.5$ or $f4.5$. These are simply half-way stations, and the doubling begins at the next opening marked on the camera.

Getting to grips with your camera

The indispensables of snapshooting are your film, your camera, and you, yourself.

The part of you that gets into the act most intimately is your hands, and the most obvious place for them *not* to be is over the lens. To avoid the embarrassment of discovering too late that a finger had dangled down into the lens' field of view, make certain when snapping that all ten of your fingers are touching the camera body.

Cameras vary tremendously in dimension, and each of them, like each fraternal organization, requires a different and unique grip. Instruction booklets always illustrate the most efficient, comfortable hand holds, and their recommendations should be followed right down to the last finger.

For the most stable possible snapping position, stand with your feet well spaced. On windy days, it's advisable to seek out a wall or tree to lean against for extra support. And always squeeze the camera button gently—punching it jars the camera and makes pictures fuzzy.

If you ever discover yourself in a snapshot situation which demands a shutter time of 1/25 second or longer, one good trick is to brace your camera against a fence, an automobile fender, or any other steady support. If you get into situations like this often, add a Kodak Flexiclamp to your photographic kit. This inexpensive, pocket-size gadget screws into the camera tripod socket and will fasten onto almost any object.

While it is desirable to hold eye-level cameras firmly against your cheek, twin-lens reflex cameras, the ones sighted at waist level, should be held away from the body. Breathing motion can often cause noticeable camera movement. Another method of keeping your twin-lens reflex camera steady while snapping is to hold it down so that the neckstrap remains taut.

WHAT WENT WRONG?

UNDEREXPOSURE

If only light-colored areas of the subject are visible and the negative looks transparent, too little light reached the film. Causes? Outdoors, the amount of daylight was too little for your camera or camera settings to produce a good negative. Indoors, either your estimate of flash distance was too great, you were using an incorrect flash lamp, or your batteries were past their peak.

OVEREXPOSURE

Too much light causes a print with no really dark areas and a negative that's extremely black. Outdoors, it may be due to incorrect settings or use of Tri-X Film in a box camera. Indoors, the cause might be the wrong kind of flash lamp or flashing your subject from too close.

OUT OF FOCUS OR TOO MUCH ACTION

When the background is sharp but the subject fuzzy, it can be a result of the subject moving too rapidly to be "stopped" by the shutter or of incorrect focusing. In a close-up, though, the problem is generally one of focusing. With adjustable cameras, measure close-up distances carefully; with box cameras, use a Kodak Close-Up Attachment for anything nearer than six feet.

CAMERA MOVEMENT

If all parts of the picture are fuzzy, the camera was moved as the picture was being snapped. This traces back to a sharp jab at the camera button. The easiest cure is perfecting a gentle trigger squeeze.

OVEREXPOSURE

Pale colors indicate overexposure. Again, make certain you are following the daylight recommendations listed in the film instruction sheet and, in your flash shots, that you aren't employing either an incorrect lamp or firing it too close to the subject.

UNDEREXPOSURE

Dark, doleful colors are due to underexposure. Outdoors, make certain that the kind of daylight always matches up with the capabilities of your camera and/or camera settings. Indoors, you may be overestimating flash distance, using a type of flash lamp that doesn't fully synchronize, or be the victim of old, tired flash batteries.

TYPE A OR B FILM EXPOSED TO DAYLIGHT

Type A or B films are designed to view the world in the relatively yellow light of incandescent tungsten lamps. When exposed by the comparatively blue illumination of daylight they produce pictures in which this blueness engulfs all the colors. These films, however, can be successfully shot under daylight with recommended filters.

DAYLIGHT TYPE FILM EXPOSED BY CLEAR FLASH

To produce pleasant color reproduction, Daylight Type films must be exposed by the comparatively blue illumination of daylight If pictures are made on them by the yellowish light of clear flash lamps, these pictures will have an unattractive orange look. For flash snapshots with Daylight Type films, use blue flash lamps.

17

FROM SHARP PICTURES TO GOOD PICTURES

If every sharp, clear, recognizable snapshot was also a really good snapshot, we could inscribe

THE END

right here and devote the remaining 174 pages to a learned commentary on yodeling in the Austrian Tyrol or some similarly nonphotographic topic. Strict adherence to the few precepts set down on the previous pages is all that's really necessary for achieving sharp pictures nearly all of the time. Any further exposition would simply be frosting on the cake.

But the difference between a sharp picture and a good picture often is an appreciable one. Certainly, if you went about your snap-shooting business continually making well exposed photographs, some of them would be quite good. The workings of the law of averages guarantees this. By merely absorbing a few basic ideas about pictures, though, you can raise the level of your results considerably.

There's no denying that many good pictures have their source in something that's beyond the range of instruction. Often, it's pure luck; often, it's the inborn ability of the photographer to recognize a promising picture situation; often, it's the same kind of ability acquired through experience.

But certain simple principles do exist which can convert what might have been an ordinary snapshot into one that's interesting not only to the person who took it, but to almost anyone. These are ideas which you can automatically incorporate into your thinking every time you peer into your viewfinder. They aren't complex and they don't require the kind of fussing that turns fun into a grim, sober, painstaking business. Once you've consciously experimented with them a bit, you'll find them so normal that they'll be second nature whenever you haul your camera out and slip a roll of film into it.

This is basically a horizontal picture. The figures and their reflections form a strong, natural, horizontal line. If snapped vertically, you not only amputate legs but also acquire waste space above and below.

Vertical or horizontal?

The picture area should, as much as possible, be filled with picture material. Holding a camera vertically to snap someone in a reclining position is likely to leave about four-fifths of the snapshot as bare of interest as a week-old savings account. Whenever you make a picture, you're paying for the entire film area. You might as well, then, crowd as much picture interest into it as you can without running over at the edges.

Every camera that shoots rectangular pictures can be held either horizontally or vertically, but many snap-shooters become so accustomed to holding it in one way that they tend to treat it as if it was locked in that position. The format, though, should always match the kind of subject material. Illustrations in magazines and books will provide a good guide to the circumstances in which vertical is more effective and those in which horizontal is best.

19

Bright sunlight, particularly near the end of the day, creates warm, brilliant colors in correctly exposed color transparencies.

Colors on bright and dull days

On a bright day, colors look bright. On a dull day, they look dull. Our eye sees this and our mind recognizes it, but not to the same extent as color film does. This occurs chiefly because we recall how red a red shirt looked on a sunny day and transfer some of that remembered redness into the dull version observed on a dull day. Color film, however, has no memory. When correctly exposed, it shows things as it sees them.

Cloudy, dull, overcast days cause colors to be lacking in brilliance but often produce pictures having a pleasant, cool effect.

This isn't necessarily bad. It *can* be annoying. Most color snapshots are made in the hope of obtaining bright colors and, under a leaden sky, this is pretty much impossible without spoiling the naturalness of the picture. If this were not true, though, it would be quite difficult to distinguish between snapshots made under different kinds of daylight. Sometimes, too, color snapshots made on cloudy days have an attractiveness and mood that would be entirely lacking if shot by bright sunshine. Many of the illustrations in this book demonstrate the point.

21

Frame devices

Picture frames are, perhaps, one of the least truly functional kinds of furniture in a home. They do, however, have a purpose, even if most people don't consciously think of it when using them. Frames set off pictures from whatever surrounds them—in most cases, a wall.

Photographically, frame devices are helpful for just about the same reason. They tend to center interest on the subject by separating that subject from whatever surrounds it. In a sense, they contribute a feeling of unity. If the frame devices are much nearer the camera than the subject they also communicate a feeling of depth and are one of the best means of achieving this.

Natural frames can be found almost anywhere. Trees, fences, windows, and bridges are examples of familiar objects that make first-rate photographic frames.

Overhanging branches contribute a frame for scenic shots and also a feeling of depth.

Often, a picture can consist mostly of frame as this one does. It depends upon whether the center of interest is really attractive or interesting enough to merit it.

Unusual frames make for unusual snapshots. One like this demands considerable imagination but produces a picture which instantly captures the attention and, because of the boy's expression, holds it, as well.

23

Keep it simple

A simple statement of fact, whether orally or visually, is often the most persuasive. Straightforward arrangements attract the eye because they express their content quickly. In pictures of people or things, simplicity is a true virtue.

The line of action

Horizontal lines communicate rest. They are the man stretched out, asleep on his back, or the horizon of a quiet meadow. Diagonal lines mean action. They are the athlete straining forward for an extra measure of speed or the passenger engine leaning against a curved section of track.

Diagonal lines stimulate picture interest. They lend an air of something going on, of force, of implied movement. Not every kind of picture subject lends itself to a diagonal treatment, but in a surprisingly large number of situations it is possible and will give you a better snapshot.

25

How Close?

In a way, taking pictures involves one of the skills of a butcher. You have to know how much to cut off.

Pictures should almost always be made from as close as possible without eliminating any part of the subject that's important to the snapshot or any part of the background that contributes to the meaning or the mood of it.

When arranging things in your viewfinder, always ask yourself, "What should this be a picture of?" Then include only the elements you find in your answer.

The back of a mother's head isn't nearly as interesting as the front of a baby's face. Although you can always make prints later from a small, cropped area of a good negative, it's much easier to do your cropping with your camera by shooting the picture from close-up.

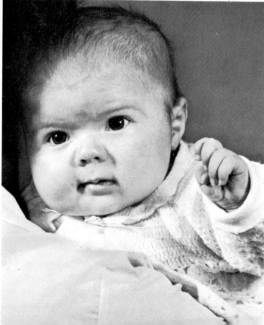

The picture here is one of a kitten in a water pitcher, but three-quarters of the area in the lower version is taken up by background that's entirely extraneous. With small subjects like this, it's a good rule of thumb to snap from as close as your camera permits.

27

A feeling of depth

Photographers, both amateur and professional, devote considerable portions of their waking, working hours to cheating the laws of physics by trying to create an atmosphere of three dimensions on a material of two.

Why? Well, we associate reality with a perception of depth, and most people want their pictures to look real.

This is best achieved by having familiar and recognizable objects at varying distances from the camera. Given the different size relationships in the snapshot and its own knowledge of actual size, the viewer's mind will do the rest.

Recognizable objects at different distances from the camera establish a strong feeling of depth. The massiveness of the statue in the foreground is particularly helpful in simulating the third dimension.

When the same kind of object, repeated over and over again, trails off into the distance, it also contributes a remarkable illusion of depth.

29

This is a fine snapshot of a very typical slice of life. If it has a fault, it's that the background is rather distracting so that the activity tends to be lost against it. Results would probably be better if the photographer had changed position by 180 degrees.

Backgrounds

Your camera always looks beyond a picture subject, and so should you. A detail-filled, distracting, "busy" background will make any picture look sloppy. It also detracts from the subject by not permitting a viewer's eye to concentrate on it.

When you see such a background in your viewfinder, sometimes it's only necessary to shift your snapping position to acquire a plain, simple, less distracting one. If this isn't the case, you can almost always shoot upward at the subject so that the horizon and sky become the background. Other likely backdrop candidates are water, a beach, grass, and trees.

Sometimes a poor background is virtually unavoidable. Owners of adjustable cameras can cope with such a situation by employing an equivalent exposure with a large lens opening so that everything in front of and behind the subject will become, to the film, fuzzy and indistinct.

The best snapshot backgrounds are generally plain ones. The sky is fine for an airborne skier; the water, for an amiable pelican. When there's an unavoidably "busy" backdrop, a wide lens opening will turn it into out-of-focus fuzziness.

Snapshots of BABIES

*Babies can be awful. They come home from the
hospital with all kinds of atrocious manners as
standard equipment. They live by their stomachs
instead of by the clock; they are not
housebroken; they require an
enormous amount of carrying,
dressing, undressing, feeding, and
amusing; they have no command at all
of the English language.*

   *Still, babies do have some redeeming
qualities. They are the best possible
excuse for having a camera and using it
frequently. Memorable, delightful
baby pictures are remarkably easy to make
chiefly because the subject matter is so expressive,
co-operative, and, when all the goods and bads are
balanced up, just plain wonderful.*

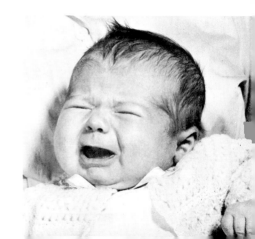

An important year with a very young lady. Only frequent and regular picture taking can provide a memorable, irreplaceable photographic chronicle like this one.

When and with what

Some years ago *Life* magazine offered a tribute to a Memphis newspaper photographer who, at the birth of his son, vowed to snap a different picture of him every day of his initial year. Three hundred and sixty-five snapshots later, he had compiled a remarkable document but was, admittedly, pretty exhausted by the whole affair.

While such a Spartan regimen is easily and thankfully avoidable, it is desirable to have some sort of regular picture-taking program. Babies are the most contrary possible beings and if you ignore, for a couple of weeks, the high comedy of first attempts at self-feeding, chances are that by the time you haul out your camera, the chore is being handled with near-professional competence.

A good snapshot schedule would require some sort of picture-taking session once a week for the first six months and then every second or third week till the first birthday. To make certain that impromptu opportunities between planned sessions don't slip away, cultivate the habit of keeping a loaded camera in some convenient place around your home, and be sure it's one that Mom, as well as Dad, can operate since so much of baby activity that's really worth shooting occurs when only she is on the scene. This all may sound like a staggering amount of photographic activity, but infants change so rapidly that it provides the only means of assuring that no significant phase of babyhood goes unrecorded.

For most picture taking of this sort, black-and-white film will usually be the best bet. There's no denying that a really good color picture of a baby possesses an appeal and charm far beyond the scope of black-and-white, but to obtain worthwhile baby shots you must shoot a lot. Expression is all-important and nothing is more transient than a baby's expression. Not only does black-and-white film prove the most economical kind, a factor that enables you to use it with greater liberality, but its enormous exposure latitude makes it the most error-proof as well.

Color, of course, shouldn't be neglected. Every month or so, and on important occasions, do your snapping in color for the special magic that only color provides.

In indoor snapping, the most universally applicable source of illumination is flash. The light from a flash lamp, by the way, cannot possibly harm a baby's eyes but a damaged lamp certainly may and a shield, such as a Kodak Flashguard, is a highly recommended safety measure.

Even box cameras can get many fine flashless indoor snapshots with Kodak Verichrome Pan Film when the baby is placed in direct sunlight near a window. Adjustable cameras are capable of indoor pictures without any special lighting in an even wider range of circumstances when you use light-sensitive film called Kodak Tri-X Pan Film or Kodak High Speed Ektachrome Film. There's more about this in the chapter beginning on page 149.

In the hospital

Unhappily, all babies aren't born beautiful. Although some will be round and pink from the beginning, the majority turn out red, wrinkly, and rumpled.

This shouldn't discourage you from snapping your latest arrival. There's a miraculous newness to every baby and, if nothing else, your hospital shots will provide a startling comparison three weeks later when Nature has turned red to pink, erased all splotchiness, and smoothed out the wrinkles.

The nursery nurse will usually either hold a newborn up for a few snapshots or move its bassinet to some convenient location. Do your shooting from as near as your camera will permit. With box cameras, a Kodak Close-Up Attachment over the lens is virtually an essential. If shoot-

A citizen only moments old can be photographed close-up by flash in his nursery bassinet if you cover the flash holder with two thicknesses of white handkerchief.

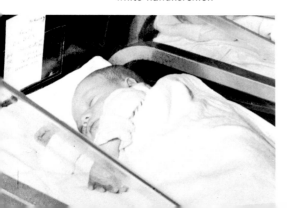

36

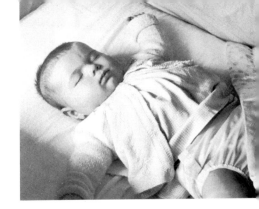

Morning. An east window. An infant lulled to sleep by the warm sunshine pouring through. In direct light like this, you can make the picture in exactly the same way you'd make an outdoor snapshot.

ing by flash, make sure to cover your flashholder with two thicknesses of white handkerchief. Without a contrivance like this, the nearness of the flash to the subject would be likely to cause an overexposure. And if separated from your baby by the nursery's glass wall, snap from an oblique angle to the glass rather than head on. This avoids disturbing reflections from the flash.

Early weeks at home

A baby's first six weeks are largely an unrelieved program of sleeping and eating, but no photographic chronicle of babyhood should ignore either.

For the softest, easiest, and best naptime pictures, roll the crib or bassinet up against a window that's flooded with direct sunlight. If the sun is really bright, you can snap away just as though you were outdoors.

Since this and nearly all baby photos ought to be made close up, it's desirable to have some reliable guide as to how close you can get. The distance for box cameras with

Good baby pictures should usually be snapped from as close as your camera permits. For an always-present reminder, attach to the bottom of the camera a string with a knot tied at the nearest focusing distance.

37

a Kodak Close-Up Attachment is 3½ feet; for adjustable-focus cameras it will be marked on the focusing ring. Unless your camera has a rangefinder device, cut a string the exact length of the closest focusing distance and fasten it to the bottom of the camera. It makes a handy measuring device whenever you get into close-up range.

A fine opportunity for wide-awake snapshots stems from that essential follow-up to eating, burping. Whether the lap method or the over-the-shoulder technique is employed, keep your camera handy. As with all flash snapping from 3½ feet or nearer, the reflector should be covered with two thicknesses of white handkerchief.

A pair of milestones that deserve snapshot attention are a baby's first experience with solid foods and his or her initial garbing in a real little suit or dress. Both are close-up situations but particularly the food adventure and its likelihood of varied facial expression.

By far the biggest daily event in any tiny infant's life is his bath. For one of your planned snapshot sessions try to cover all phases including undressing, washing, drying, and postbath operations.

When an infant reaches the two-month mark, he or she is about ready to be propped up for a good look at the world around. This is a fine time to keep your camera busy,

Babies really love life as soon as they're able to get a real look at things. Whether it's the pleasure of sitting upright or the daily delight of a bath, catch the expression from close-up.

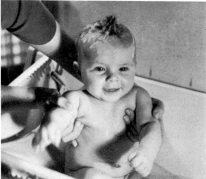

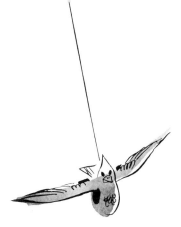

A bird can be one of creation's marvels, though it only spins in circles. Again, shoot from as close as possible and cover the flash holder with two thicknesses of white handkerchief.

especially if you've procured one of the many crib mobiles now on the market. These devices, with their slowly circling birds and butterflies, are sure to elicit photogenic responses. An excellent way of catching them is to shoot right through the mobile. It won't matter if the figures on the mobile are too close to the camera to be in focus, just as long as the baby's face is.

From three months onward

These are the days in which babies become capable of really doing things. Although not perhaps ready to solo in a high chair or baby seat, they manage admirably when aided by a couple of pillows.

Given a toy, preferably a small one that won't get in the way, an upright infant will supply all the snapshot material your camera can handle. Whenever you have control over the location of the picture subject as you do here, choose some place that provides a plain, uncluttered background. "Busy" backgrounds with lots of distracting detail make your picture look sloppy and draw interest away from the subject.

When interest in a toy palls, you can try having some-one standing alongside the camera perform a little vaude-ville entertainment for the benefit of the small fry. Such diversions as the construction of a tower of blocks and its inevitable collapse seldom fail to produce picture-worthy material.

Initial stabs at self-feeding are a prime opportunity for color snapping, providing that you can muster sufficient self-control. If you do use color film, serve the baby red or pink puddings for the happiest results.

The age of discovery

When a baby comes face to face with a dog for the first time or lays hands on his first lollipop, only a single snap-shot of the occasion would be as inadequate as a parasol in a monsoon. Any event that's likely to generate a story, even as simple a story as one of these, demands more than one picture.

A series of pictures actually is doubly desirable when covering the exciting, exacting, and exasperating exploits of the very young. First, a series insures that you capture every snapshot-worthy bit of business integral to the story. In addition, by shooting a series you enhance the possibility that one of your pictures will turn out to be something more than just a good, normal snapshot of a baby. Even professional photographers who earn their livings kid-snapping admit that the law of averages is one of their most dependable allies.

Not all good baby pictures show the baby's face. This one was snapped by the existing illu-mination in the room. Exposure with Tri-X Film was 1/50, f/3.5.

40

The difference between an expressive picture and
an ordinary snapshot can simply be the presence
of someone to attract the baby's attention.

The wonders of household exploration revealed when a
child learns to crawl are another fine opportunity for a
snapshot series. So is the discovery of mirrors. Seat a
baby in front of a mirror for the first time and you have
as near an ideal subject as most snapshooters will ever
enjoy.

There's one special wrinkle to mirror shots. Make certain when you check the picture in your viewfinder that
you can't see yourself in the mirror. This is particularly
important when snapping by flash since if you and the
camera are visible, there'll be a huge glare spot resulting

Some boys like cats; some boys like their bottle; some like both. It's the reaction to the cat, though, that makes the picture.

Baby pictures must be made at baby level even if it means, as here, stretching out on the floor.

Crawling opens a world of exploration. Whether indoors or out, your camera should follow.

that will spoil your snapshot. The most desirable snapping angle is at about 45° to the mirror with the baby facing generally in your direction.

When babies and other babies, or babies and animals get together, it's a photographer's field day. Household pets seem instinctively gentle with small children and there's little cause for apprehension when they get in close proximity. When the animals are puppies or kittens, expect a display of mutual curiosity and keep your camera down low enough (even if it means sprawling out at ground level with attendant loss of dignity) to get a good view of the ensuing fun.

Sometime within the last half of their first year, many little boys are brought, some kicking and screaming, to the barber shop for their first shearing. An event of such proportion should always be photographed and flash will do the job dependably. The only possible problem is that if the young man is one of the minority that takes issue with the whole haircutting idea, flash may aggravate the situation. Here owners of adjustable cameras have an edge

because in any well-lighted barbering establishment they can probably record everything without flash by employing Kodak Tri-X Film and setting their camera lens to its widest opening.

The same situation occurs when small boys, and small girls as well, journey off to the local supermarket for their initial shopping expedition. Flash is an easy way of recording their reactions but shooting by existing light with Tri-X Film is even better if your camera is the adjusting kind. A setting of 1/50, *f*/3.5 will give good results in most stores.

Sharing your baby-snapshot bounty

Everyone, it seems, loves babies and pictures of babies. Good snapshots make welcome enclosures in letters and yield enlargements which are fine potential gifts. Grouped into albums, they are deeply appreciated by relatives and friends. For widest possible circulation, though, there's nothing quite like a photographic Christmas greeting and on page 185 you'll find all the details.

Snapshots of

CHILDREN

*At the quiet time that inevitably comes to even
the most frenzied day, the children finally off to bed
and the arena of their activities still in disorder,
it may be difficult for any pair of exhausted parents
to conceive of the growing up process
as anything but an unmixed blessing.*

*Somehow, though, this all changes as the stages
of growing up pass by and leave behind them
nothing more of the toddler, the kindergarten
scholar, the Space Cadet, the Red Cross nurse,
the summer camper, and the intense teen-ager
than a scant few souvenirs, a tangle of memory,
and some snapshots.*

*But these snapshots, if there are sufficient and
the right kind of them, can be your strongest
foothold in yesterday. The kids in photographs
never grow up.*

*Making memorable snapshots of growing children
is no more difficult than snapshots of babies.
The only difference is that the older kids
just move around faster.*

On natural-looking snapshots and birdies

A large proportion of parents, grandparents, fond aunts and uncles have been snapping pictures for years and years under the assumption that all picture subjects should be treated as habitual bird watchers. "Now, now, look at the birdie," they will coax, and the resulting snapshots generally have all the natural sparkle of a police department mug shot.

When there's a child in front of your camera lens, you nearly always have a choice between a picture that will show what the child *looks* like or what he *is* like. This may seem similar to asking if you'd prefer your tomatoes to be red or to be round. Of course you usually want them to be both, but a snapshot of a child can't always span the two options nor should it.

How often have you been shown a birdie-type photo of a small boy which was accompanied by a story something like this?

"Oh yes, this was snapped of Tommy on the Decoration Day picnic two years ago when he was leaning over the dock trying to catch fish with his hands and fell into the lake."

46

Was the picture you saw characteristically Tommy? Wouldn't you rather have seen one of him actually engaged in the fateful fishing mission, being dragged out of the lake, or standing by during the removal of his soaked clothing even if none of these shots had a full-face view of the boy?

Actually, some of the most wonderful snapshots of kids are not at all flattering. Many of them don't even include the child's face. Impossible? Not a bit. The evidence is right here among the illustrations.

In the long run, the photos of children most likely to become treasured are those in which the kids are strenuously engaged in the business of being themselves. There certainly is a place for snapshots made primarily to show what a child looks like and some easy but effective ways to keep them pleasing and natural.

But by all means let's take that old, worn-out birdie; stuff it; and retire it to the museum shelf alongside all the other relics of days gone by.

47

No stiff birdie-watching here. These are simply small boys and girls caught in the wonderful business of being themselves. Pictures of this sort are among the very easiest to make. Little children aren't at all awed by a camera. It's just a matter of remembering to keep your camera at hand and of pressing the button at the right moment.

Whether it's splashing through a pile of golden autumn leaves or adopting airs suitable to clothing pilfered from an attic trunk, kids never lack for occupation. If you take advantage of their manifold activities, neither will your trusty camera.

Ways and means of informal snapshots

The best informal pictures of children are often taken when many parents would least expect the situation to yield exceptional snapshot opportunities. Looking at photos of this sort, it's easy to assume they are always snapped by professionals whose every waking moment is spent eye-to-viewfinder, something you certainly don't have time to do. Only they aren't.

Naturally, wonderful pictures of kids are only achieved by spending a great deal of time with kids. For most parents this is not only easy but virtually inescapable.

Also, to take advantage of a picture opportunity, you must have a camera at the right place and time. This sometimes isn't so easy. Keeping your own camera at hand whenever you're likely to be around children is a worthwhile habit but one that requires dogged developing. One thing it doesn't require, though, is that you become so preoccupied with picture taking that it dominates all other considerations. Instead, merely use your camera to take advantage of those situations which, in the past, evoked a vain, "Gee, wouldn't that make a cute snapshot."

By the way, good snapshot situations aren't always readily apparent. Many of them are bound to pass unnoticed There's no trick or formal course of instruction that will help here, but you will begin reducing your number of misses by just noting the kind of photographs reproduced in picture magazines, in advertisements, and in books like this one.

Perhaps most important of all, make certain that your own children are so accustomed to being photographed that the appearance of a camera won't freeze them into stiff self-consciousness. Again, carrying and using your camera frequently in connection with family activities will usually take care of this. Once you've accomplished this, try hanging around the fringes of solely juvenile activities and the snapshots you're likely to get should be among the best in your collection.

Surprisingly, people who follow a snapshooting program of this sort don't necessarily spend any more money on picture taking than those whose approach is more casual. But they certainly do make better pictures.

How to pose children

Head clamps, arm clamps, and hand clamps ring more of the medieval torturer than the nineteenth-century photographic studio. During the dim early days of picture taking, though, such items of hardware were hardly less indispensible to the man behind the camera than the black plush cloth he hid beneath. Exposure times were often as tedious as five minutes long and the photographer's subject had to be shackled into a rock-steady attitude. Some of the grim portraits that resulted undoubtedly bespeak itches going unscratched and other by-products of immobility.

To a parent occasionally desirous of posing a pleasant picture of his or her own jet-propelled small fry, clamps may not, on reflection, seem such a bad idea. Fortunately there are some reliable ways and means of accomplishing all this without resort to manacles or to athletic prodigiosity.

First, any attempt to brave it alone would merely be a display of unmerited optimism. Especially with small children, always enlist the aid of an accomplice who can stand outside the picture area, talk to the child, help stimulate little bits of action, and keep the child's attention away from your camera. Good snapshots hardly ever result when a youngster is staring squarely into the lens. By shifting the location of your helper and promoting a steady flow of conversation between helper and subject, you'll not only be able to have the child facing in any direction you wish but also be likely to obtain bright, animated expressions.

50

Sometimes a prop isn't necessary for a posed picture; sometimes it helps a great deal. When in doubt, though, try one.

Older kids usually love to clown for the camera. Exhibit A—this version of "In Philadelphia nearly everyone reads the *Bulletin*."

Use props whenever you can. Any object that captivates or absorbs a child's interest will help you produce snapshots capturing that special delight or absorption. A few of the most commonly and successfully used props for little children are toys, musical instruments, small animals, articles of clothing, books, food, and all kinds of ticking, moving, or flexible gadgets.

Keep your prop out of sight until you're all set up and ready to snap. Then let your helper hand it to the child. The initial expression is often the best picture and it will be an unhappy snapshooter who views it while loading his camera, hunting for a package of flash lamps, or actually giving the prop to the child himself.

Oftentimes the prop may be so fraught with interest that your small subject won't require any further prompting from you to create ample snapshot material. On the other hand, your helper should be ready to suggest activities such as, "Listen to the clock tick," or "Hug your dolly," or "Try Daddy's hat on."

A boy, his spaniel, and the wonderful exhilaration of an early spring day. Sometimes, as here, wide expanses of background help give a picture a special feeling, even though most shots of children should be made close-up.

Television makes a first-rate photographic prop. Any youngster particularly fascinated by a TV show will bubble over with varied responses to it. To catch them, just station yourself off to one side of the set and snap away. Adjustable-type cameras again provide an edge in this kind of snapping. With Kodak Tri-X Pan Film or High Speed Ektachrome Film in a daylit room, they can be used to shoot pictures without flash and will avoid its inescapable disturbance. Use an exposure meter.

Outdoors, too, the use of props is equally helpful. Flowers or snowballs, depending upon the season, can furnish enough diversion for a good snapshot and even just a fence to climb or lean on will often be sufficient to give your picture a charming naturalness.

Older children, while easier to direct, are a great deal less easy to divert. Approach them with a camera and there's no disguising what you have in mind. Props, though, are still beneficial, not so much to draw the subject's attention away from the camera but to give the picture a reason for being. Placing a squirmy kitten in the hands of a teen-age girl may evoke an entirely different reaction than if you placed the same kitten in the hands of a three-year-old, but it *will* evoke a response and, chances are, that response will be the best ingredient of your picture.

52

The helper idea is also effective with older children, even if it accomplishes nothing more than drawing their eyes away from the camera. The reaction to a gibe or joke will always be much warmer and more natural than anything you'll obtain by begging, "C'mon now, lets' have a smile."

Kid close-ups

Ask a professional photographer how close you should be to snap a child's picture and, if he's in a particularly enigmatic mood, he may say, "Close enough," smile, and wander off to enjoy his little joke in some quiet corner.

Despite the scarcity of feet and inches in this sort of reply, "Close enough," is actually close enough to a really helpful answer, especially if you append, " . . . to see what's going on."

Any kind of snapshot, but especially a snapshot of a child, should always be snapped from as close as you possibly can without amputating any important part of the picture.

Let's say that the reason for a picture is entirely concentrated in a child's face. The child might be sniffing a flower, popping bubble gum, or reacting to a new food. The likeliest place for your camera to be is just as close

If all the interest is concentrated in a face, snap from 3½ feet (with box cameras, use a Close-Up Attachment); if full figures are required, step back a pace or two.

as it is capable of making a sharp picture. With box cameras this distance is around 6 feet; slip a Kodak Close-Up Attachment over the lens and the distance shifts in to a more desirable 3½ feet. Adjustable cameras nearly always focus to 3½ feet, many of them down to 2 feet. At this range, no matter which kind of camera you have, the zone of sharp focus is rather narrow. Camera-to-subject distance should be measured carefully.

When the picture situation depends on what the entire child is up to, step back so that you can see the entire child in your viewfinder. If there's any chance that your busy subject might change position, back up an extra foot or two to allow a safety zone.

At distances nearer than 6 feet, owners of adjustable cameras have a special trick at their disposal for minimizing cluttered, distracting backgrounds and concentrating attention on the subject in an unusually attractive way. This trick, called "selective focus," produces a snapshot in which everything in front of and behind the subject is as much out of focus as possible.

This effect results from focusing carefully on the subject and then using an equivalent exposure that has a wide lens opening. If, for example, you were shooting with

54

Kodacolor Film on a bright, sunny day, the basic exposure would be 1/50, *f* 11; to administer the "selective focus" treatment, you might instead set your camera at 1/200, *f* 5.6 (four times as large a lens opening with a shutter time only one-fourth as long).

Often the meaning of a picture will depend to some degree upon the background and when this is the case, include as much of it as you need but no more. Generally speaking, snapshots of this kind should have sharply focused backgrounds and so, with adjustable cameras, follow the basic exposure given in the film instructions. These basic exposures always have a small lens opening, and small lens openings carry with them a wide range of sharp focus.

Snapshots of children can be close and sharp and still be entirely useless. This most often occurs when five-foot- or six-foot-tall adults stand as stiff-backed as Grenadier Guards and snap down at three-foot-tall kids who don't happen, at the moment, to be wearing stilts. There's hardly ever an interesting expression on top of a child's head. Keep your camera down low, even if it means bending, kneeling, stooping, squatting, or sprawling.

If a picture is accidentally or unavoidably snapped from too far away, there still is one last resort, providing that the film is a negative type like any black-and-white film or

These are both fine snapshots, but the one of the girl has an undistracting, out-of-focus background, while the shot of the boy's tender-tough treatment of the kitten is marred by a sharp, cluttered background.

like Kodacolor Film. First, make certain that the child is sharp and the expression is good. Then take the negative to your Kodak dealer and explain that you'd like a print or enlargement made from only part of the negative area rather than the entire negative. He'll tell you which partial area sizes are standard and will help you mark your negative in the correct manner.

Even when corrective measures like these are available, though, it's still a good idea to fall back on them only in the most dire circumstances. Try to shoot it right—that is, close enough—the first time around.

Children in action

In the hard school of parenthood, a cardinal principle learned early in the course is that a period of sudden silence is likely to be a portent of impending calamity. The natural state of a child, any age, is motion, a motion that characteristically trails behind it some sort of clatter.

Motion, then, is natural and natural snapshots are desirable. The only problem is knowing what special things to do with your camera when on the trail of a speeding small fry.

These pictures suggest action even though there's nothing moving. A box camera or an adjustable camera set at 1/50 could make snapshots like these easily.

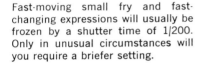

Fast-moving small fry and fast-changing expressions will usually be frozen by a shutter time of 1/200. Only in unusual circumstances will you require a briefer setting.

Cameras are capable of making sharp pictures of anything from a jack-in-the-box to a jet. The lone requirement is that there be no substantial amount of movement during the interval in which the film is being exposed. Getting a sharp action snapshot, therefore, depends on a pair of factors: how rapidly the subject is moving, and how long the camera shutter remains open.

The shutter time of most box cameras is fixed at about 1/50 second. This is an extremely brief slice of time, briefer than any stop watch can measure accurately. It isn't brief enough, however, to freeze any but the slowest sort of motion. Still, box cameras, with the proper guidance, will make fine action shots.

In many fast action situations only a comparatively small part of your young subject will actually be moving. When a girl swings at a badminton bird, chances are that all of her except her arm is pretty much motionless. The same is true when a youthful handyman saws a board or pounds a nail. Snapping with a box camera will yield perfectly sharp pictures except in the area of motion and here the blur tends to communicate something of the true

action. Often it provides a better snapshot than one in which the motion is frozen. There are dozens of box camera opportunities like this and even if you may not be certain of the result, it pays to take a chance.

Another significant point to remember when trying to make action snapshots with any camera, but particularly a box camera, is that a moving object, whether it's a toddler on a tricycle or a diesel express train, shows less apparent motion if it is coming directly toward you than if it is viewed from the side. Whenever your subject is on the move, always locate yourself so that you'll be getting the action head-on.

These same ideas are equally applicable to adjustable cameras when a shutter time of 1/50 second is set. One of the nice things about adjustable cameras, though, is that they adjust and one of the things on them that adjusts is the shutter time. By employing some equivalent exposure having a shutter time of 1/200 second you can snap nearly all ordinary, around-the-house action without any blurring from the motion. In 1/200 second the film gets a much briefer look at the picture than at 1/50, and most things that move enough in 1/50 to cause a blurring don't move any appreciable amount in 1/200. Bright sunlight lens openings that go with a 1/200 or 1/250 second shutter time for average subjects are:

Kodak Films	Lens Openings	Kodak Films	Lens Openings
Panatomic-X	$f/8$	Ektachrome	$f/5.6$
Verichrome Pan	$f/11$	Ektachrome-X	$f/8$
Tri-X Pan	$f/22$	Kodachrome II	$f/5.6$
Kodacolor	$f/5.6$	Kodachrome-X	$f/8$
Kodacolor-X	$f/8$	High Speed Ektachrome	$f/16$

You can find the lens openings for 1/200 second under other lighting conditions by mental arithmetic or from the Kodak Snapshot Dial.

Natural-looking pictures are likely to be products of natural situations. No amount of coaxing could draw as excited an expression on a young lady's face as a few jounces on a pony's back.

Snapshots of

GROWN-UPS

*All the movie monsters laid out fang to forelock
have never cut as wide a swath of terror
through the ranks of humanity as the humble little
snapshot camera. Merely unmask a camera's
Cyclopean eye among almost any group and
strong men wither, ladies pale, and the entire
gathering promptly assumes the relaxed air
of a convention in a wax museum.*

*   The perfunctory efforts of medical science to
unravel this riddle have consistently been balked.
It has been mentioned that a manufacturer of
practical jokes did, at one time, market a
remarkably realistic facsimile of a box camera
with a gadget like a jack-in-the-box which
hurtled out of the "lens" when a button was pushed.
This, however, was many years ago and its
alarming effect should be entirely dissipated by now.
This vast, unfathomable terror in the presence of
such an innocent device is a constant source of
anguish to the man behind the camera. It often
forces him to employ the guile of an
espionage agent to get a pleasant
looking snapshot. Before a wave of
defeatism settles over this page, let it
be stated that life for the snapshooter
can be, if not beautiful, at least livable.
For further details, merely continue
to the next paragraph.*

Preoccupied people are among the best of picture subjects. The same goes for their cats, too. The pleasant lighting for this snapshot is open shade.

Getting subjects to relax

For more years than most can remember, the typical snapshot of a grown-up shows him or her in a pose that would make the commander of a firing squad lick his chops appreciatively. Whenever someone brandishes a camera, the average adult seems to grit his teeth, snap out a mental "Attention!" to himself, and brace for the ordeal.

Here are a few of the most common and effective antidotes to this sort of situation:

Be sneaky. Shoot your picture before your intended victim knows that you and your camera are on the premises. Even better, shoot when your subject is so engrossed in some personal activity that he won't notice your photographic activity. This nearly always enables you to obtain natural snapshots. Unfortunately, it has the limiting factor that unless you carry your own portable duck blind or are naturally adept at camouflage, it's often difficult to get as close as you'd like without breaking the spell.

Ah, the joys of complete relaxation! Pictures like this aren't usually made to flatter the subject. It's more likely that the intent was blackmail.

62

A sitting-down subject nearly always seems more relaxed than one who is standing. Overcast days provide a light ideal for snapshots of people.

If you can't be sneaky, be persuasive. Talk your subject into assuming or resuming some sort of activity just for purposes of a snapshot. This way, you can snap from close-up. If your subject seems self-conscious or stares blankly into the camera lens, enlist the help of someone to stand off in the direction in which you'd like your subject to be looking and also relax the subject with a bit of extraneous conversation.

If sneakiness and persuasiveness don't work, take a seat. Invite your subject to sit down too. People relax more easily in a seated position than in an upright one and whether the means is a chair, a floor, the ground, or a flight of steps, chances are that you'll come up with a more pleasing snapshot than the stiff old cigar store Indian approach would yield.

If sitting isn't fitting, try leaning. Fences, trees, walls, doorways, and tables are fine leaning props. Anything at all contrived to help a subject or group loosen up will pay off in improved pictures.

Sometimes nothing'll get them to bite. The dejection of a fisherman, though, is often as worthy of a picture as his great moments of triumph and success.

63

Different kinds of daylight

Smile sweetly and repeat three times with deep conviction, "The best kind of light for picture taking is the kind I happen to have at hand." Of course, this isn't necessarily true but, like the weather, there isn't a great deal you can do about it.

Certain kinds of lighting will always produce better results in some applications than others. For the most vivid colors, color snapshots must be made on bright days; a great preponderance of scenic pictures too, whether on color film or black-and-white, will benefit from unrestricted sunshine. A hazy sun, with its absence of dark shadows and annoying glare, is ideal for photographing people, even though color snapshots are cooler looking and less brilliant than on a bright day. Cloudy conditions make for wonderful black-and-white close-ups of people and for excellent scenic pictures when the mood created by the clouds adds extra interest.

Areas dappled with patches of sunshine and shadow are tricky ones in which to photograph people. As long as there aren't any shadow areas falling across faces, though, the results can often have the pleasant, warm feeling apparent in this snapshot.

Cloudy-bright days are ideal for close-ups of people because they eliminate shadows and subject squinting. Box cameras get good results in this light with Verichrome Pan Film.

What people do is often as interesting, photographically, as what they look like. A picture like this, made in a heavy snowfall, is no trick at all, even for a box camera. And as long as the movement is either toward or away from the camera, the shutter on a box camera will be quick enough to catch it fairly sharply.

Despite these considerations, any modern flash camera, no matter how inexpensive, is fully capable of producing first rate snapshots under almost any illumination. This is extremely fortunate since only a professional photographer can usually wait for a certain sort of light before he goes out to shoot a picture. For most amateurs, a snapshot opportunity just happens and if it isn't snapped, no matter what the lighting conditions may be, chances are it won't recur tomorrow.

65

Usually you'll find that not many picture situations allow you a choice of snapping angle. Don't worry about this. Just shoot away. The talented films now available have erased most of the reasons for the old doctrine of snapping with the sun at your back. If you *can* select your own location and/or your subject's location, here are a few basic considerations.

When there's a bright sun and it is directly overhead (top lighting), dark shadows will be cast beneath eyebrows, under noses and even around cheek bones. You can see into these shadows but photographic film can't. In your pictures the shadows will appear as black blobs. The best means of eliminating them is by firing a flash lamp (a blue one with color film) when you snap your picture, a technique called fill-in flash that's described in the next section.

If the sun is shining directly into the subject's face from behind your back (front lighting), not only will the shadow. blobs probably remain but squinting becomes an additional problem. Neither will be quite as acute, however, if you shift position slightly so that the sun will be reaching your subject from just over your shoulder and off to the side a bit.

When you snap with the sun shining on your subject from one side (side lighting), there's no squinting difficulty and results tend to be quite pleasant. Half of the subject will be brightly lighted and the other half in soft shadow. With fairly exacting reversal-type color films, like Kodachrome-X and Ektachrome-X, it's a good idea to use a lens opening a full stop *wider* than you'd set for front lighting (e.g. with Kodachrome-X the basic settings for a front-lighted subject are 1/60 with the lens opening f 16; for a side-lighted subject they should be 1/60, f 11). Fill-in flash can provide an extra measure of quality in color snapshots by throwing a little additional light into the shadow side and brightening up the colors there.

With the sun behind your subject (back lighting), faces are entirely in light shadow and usually appear to have an attractive halo of brightness surrounding them. When snapping a back-lighted picture be sure that the sun isn't shining directly into the camera lens since it can splash a glare spot over the film that will spoil any picture. The earlier or later in the day that you snap, the more serious

66

Front lighting is the old "Let-the-sun-come-over-your-shoulder-and-shoot" formula. This would work out beautifully if people's faces were perfectly flat, which, of course, they aren't. Wherever parts of the face jut out—places like eyebrows, noses, chins, and cheeks—the bright sun will make heavy, unsightly black shadows.

Side lighting still can't eliminate the dark shadows that come with bright sunlight, but it moves them around to the side of the face where they aren't quite so annoying. Best results can be obtained by facing your subject so the light will just fall across his or her nose and help to illuminate the side that is away from the sun.

Back lighting allows the sun to form bright highlights on a subject's hair and shoulders. At the same time it produces a soft, even, thoroughly pleasant illumination across the face. It's essential, though, that the sun not be shining directly into the camera lens or a glare spot can result which would spoil the picture.

Side lighting with flash fill-in doesn't eliminate shadows entirely but throws enough light toward the face to brighten them up. At close-up range like this, the flash holder should be covered with three thicknesses of white handkerchief for both black-and-white films and color films, so that its light won't exceed the effect of the sun upon the face of the subject.

this glare problem will be. To get adequate exposure you will need to use a lens opening two full stops wider than for front lighting; thus with Kodachrome-X or Koda-color-X, use f 8 at 1/60 second. Back-lighted faces often appear rather dully lighted because they are entirely in shadow. If you are shooting on a beach or in some other bright surroundings, the natural reflectance will bounce enough light toward the face to remedy this; if not, fill-in flash will be helpful, particularly in color shots.

On hazy days the effect of different lighting directions is very slight and on cloudy days there's no effect at all. Box cameras can make fine black-and-white snapshots with Kodak Verichrome Pan Film on bright, hazy, and even cloudy bright days. They'll also produce good Kodacolor pictures on any sunny day, whether bright or hazy. In all other situations, when snapping people at 10 feet or closer, use flash just as you would indoors. The lone difference is that with color films blue flash lamps must be employed rather than clear lamps.

Fill-in flash: the why and how of it

Firing a flash lamp in broad daylight may seem almost like bringing a pail of your own sand to Coney Island. Certainly there's no shortage of light outdoors even on cloudy days. The simple and intriguing fact is that flash lamps are most helpful just when the sun is at its very brightest.

Sunlight casts shadows and the brighter the light, the darker the shadows. When a camera is set to make a good picture of anything directly lighted by the sun (as a box camera always is and as an adjustable camera should be if you follow the film instruction sheet recommendations), it cannot produce a picture in which the resulting shadows

68

are much more than black blobs. In scenic snapshots, this isn't an extreme liability since shadows help give shape to objects. In close-ups of people, though, heavy shadows are as welcome as beriberi.

The easiest way to avoid shadows is via the use of front lighting. Then, all the shadows will fall behind the subject where the camera can't see them. But, if shadows are undesirable, a squinting subject is even worse and squinting accompanies front lighting with annoying persistence. Since a shadow is a lesser evil than a squint, the most satisfactory stratagem is to rearrange things so that you have side lighting. This, of course, produces a situation in which half of a face is brightly lighted and the other half is in shadow.

A flash lamp (it should always be a blue one for color films), if fired from the correct distance, can brighten up the shadow area so it will be nearly as well lighted as the sunny side. Distance, though, is a vital factor. If you have your camera set for bright sun and the lamp is too close to the subject it will cause serious over-exposure.

With Kodachrome II Film, Daylight Type, the basic exposure for a bright day is $1/60$, with the lens opening f 11. If you snap from 7 feet away and flash a blue lamp alongside your camera, the subject will receive just as much light from the flash as from the sun. In the picture, then, there will be little remaining shadow at all. Since it's usually desirable to keep some trace of the shadow evident for a natural looking picture, the distances from which the flash should be fired range between 9 and 15 feet, depending upon how much shadow you'd like to keep.

Of course 9 to 15 feet from the subject is well beyond the distance from which you'd snap a close-up. To convert this fill-in idea into a useful working tool it's necessary to cover the flash-holder reflector with two thicknesses of white handkerchief. By doing this the fill-in range moves in and becomes $4\frac{1}{2}$ to $7\frac{1}{2}$ feet.

Snapshots of ANIMALS

A writer named E. B. White wrote: "Being the owner of dachshunds, to me a book on dog training becomes a volume of inspired humor. Every sentence is a riot. Some day, if I ever get a chance, I shall write a book of warning on the character and temperament of the dachshund and why he can't be trained and shouldn't be . . . When I address Fred I never have to raise either my voice or my hopes. He even disobeys me when I instruct him in something that he wants to do. And when I answer his peremptory scratch at the door and hold the door open for him to walk through, he stops in the middle and lights a cigarette, just to hold me up."*

What is distressingly true of dachshunds is equally inevitable among the entire legion of species we have invited across our doorsills and hopefully labelled domesticated. At no time is the general contrariness of these beasts as evident as when you want to snap some pictures of them. People who dote on Double-Crostics or endure long, damp hours in duck blinds without a murmur of protest find their patience torn asunder by a balky beagle.

The simple truth is that the only animal really easy to photograph is a dead animal and even one of these may hold some surprises, like a frog's galvanic leg kick or a decapitated chicken's ability to dance a jig.

*From *One Man's Meat* by E. B. White, published by Harper & Brothers.

Animals move—what to do about this

As amiably exasperating or just plain stubborn as dogs, cats, budgie-birds, and hamsters may be, it *is* possible to maneuver, coax, and cajole them into the most appealing photographic subjects in or out of captivity. The magic catalyst is patience.

Of the various problems involved in dealing with the beasties, their propensity to move around in such a thoroughly undisciplined manner towers above all others in magnitude. Unless shackled paw to fetlock or asleep (an excellent time, by the way, to shoot animal pictures), they simply will not stay where you want them to stay. When attempting to manage two or three pets, this situation is magnified geometrically instead of merely arithmetically.

Props are of enormous assistance. Tempt a dog with a rubber bone he particularly favors (one you've thoughtfully "Scotch"-taped to the floor) or a cat with a dish of milk and you can be reasonably certain, at least for a moment, that you'll be snapping an animal and not the place where an animal happened to be a few seconds ago.

With Kodacolor or black-and-white film in your camera, it's often worthwhile to arrange an animal picture in your viewfinder and then step back an extra foot or foot and a-half, focusing, of course, for the actual camera-to-subject distance. This provides a little extra margin in which the animal may move without moving out of the picture. Since prints can be made from any portion of a good negative, you can, after examining the initial prints delivered to you by your dealer, return the negatives to him and order prints or enlargements made from the partial area in which you are interested. Whether you follow this procedure or not, most of your animal snapping will be close-up and, for box cameras, this again underlines the importance of having a Kodak Close-Up Attachment.

Unhappily this freedom to use part of an original picture doesn't readily carry over to color slides. When shooting Kodachrome and Ektachrome Films, compose the picture in your viewfinder exactly as you want it to be in your slide and just hope your quarry won't budge. As with all difficult subjects, it's a good plan to snap several shots

Although these shots could have been made at box-camera shutter time (1/50 second), it's a good idea, with an adjustable camera, to use 1/100 or 1/200 as a precaution against movement.

rather than only one. It's also a good plan to approach with your camera as slowly and naturally as you can. Frightening old Towser defeats your purpose; so does provoking his curiosity to the extent that you find a large, damp tongue exploring the lens.

Shutter time must also be keyed to the distinct possibility of some subject movement. With a box camera there isn't much that can be done about this outdoors. Indoors there's a great deal. AG-1B flash lamps discharge most of their illumination in about 1/100 second. When using one of these lamps you obtain the action-stopping ability of that 1/100 even if the shutter time built into your camera is 1/50 second. The M2 lamps produce all of their light in 1/100 and can also be helpful in this regard. But before trying any kind of flash lamp, check your camera instructions to be certain it is on the recommended list. If it isn't, chances are that it flashes either before or after your shutter opens and the film gets no benefit from it. However, the most frequent cause of flash failure is stale batteries. Have them tested or replaced if in doubt.

Outdoors with an adjustable camera, settle on an equivalent exposure for your film and sunlight conditions that provides you with a shutter time of 1/250 second. Indoors, the same flash lamps that aid the box camera-ite do equally well teamed with adjustable cameras *if* those cameras synchronize with them. Again, the camera instructions will hold this sort of information.

Snapping very small beasties close-up

There are, on the shelves of photo dealers, a group of talented monocles called Kodak Portra Lenses 1+, 2+, and 3+. These Portra Lenses are indispensable to puppies and kittens even though a pup or tabby wouldn't be likely to know a Portra Lens from a "Popsicle." Their indispensability is wrapped around the fact that, when mounted over the regular lens of an adjustable camera, they enable you to snap sharp pictures much nearer to a small animal than the minimum distance on the camera's focusing scale.

For most puppies and other puppy-size fauna, a Portra Lens 1+ works out neatly since it permits snapping anywhere from within 18 to 39 inches of the subject; for kittens, birds, and smaller fry, the 2+ lens is the best investment, with its working range of 12 to 19 inches away.

Whether in abstract contemplation or serious, practical thought, a cat's activities are always interesting. The picture on the left was exposed just as an ordinary outdoor snapshot would have been.

The instruction sheet packaged with each Portra Lens lists the camera setting in feet for various close-up snapping distances within the Portra Lens' range of operation. It would tell you, for example, that if with a 1+ lens you wanted to shoot at a camera-to-subject distance of 25½ inches, the focus should be set at 6 feet. Margin for focusing error is sliver-thin in Portra Lens country and distances must be measured, not estimated or guessed.

For a pat and proven little procedure for shooting animals at ultra close-up range, try this 1-2-3 technique:

1. Have a helper hold the pup or kitten in one hand and touch a finger of the other to the exact spot where you want the animal to be when you snap.
2. Hold your camera also just where you want it for the picture. Measure the distance from the front of the Portra Lens to the finger, and adjust the camera focusing scale based on the measured distance.
3. In one swift series of motions your helper should remove his hand, drop the animal correctly faced, and you snap.

At these extremely short distances your camera lens and viewfinder lens see a slightly different picture because one is above the other. To compensate for this, arrange your subject in the viewfinder so that the bottom of the animal is right on the bottom of the viewfinder or even slightly cut off. In the picture it will appear higher up.

Snapshots of SCENERY

" . . . and as the sun sinks slowly in the West,
we bid a fond farewell to beautiful Outer Mongolia."
And as the honeyed voice also sinks slowly in the West,
the background music swells while the glorious
crimson and ocher hues of sunset arch majestically
across the screen. For bulk magnificence
and outright size, the handiwork of Nature again
proves itself in a class of its own.

Fortunately, Nature's larger wonders are among
the easiest things to photograph and, in addition,
among the easiest to photograph well. Oftentimes
the difference between ordinary and good results
may be a measure so apparently trivial it hardly seems
worth taking. Bridalveil Falls will never be mistaken
for a drippy little five-foot cataract
in any snapshot, but merely having a person
or persons in the distant foreground when you shoot it
will do more to communicate its heroic size than a
satchel full of National Park Service statistics.

While Nature's decorating scheme would be
a difficult one to improve upon even if you wanted to,
there is an awesome collection of weapons in the
snapshot arsenal for enhancing its magnificence.
It may seem curious that a circle of yellow glass over
the camera lens will often produce a superior result,
but such are the little marvels of photographic science.

Even cloud-filled skies often turn out rather flat . . .   . . . but a yellow Pictorial Filter makes this difference.

Filters for black-and-white films

When almost anyone but a hard-bitten photo bug hears the word "filter," he thinks of a device through which a liquid passes and leaves some unwanted substance behind. Photographic filters operate in almost exactly the same way except that light is the commodity being filtered.

Filters for black-and-white snapping exist chiefly because some things appear different to the human eye than they do to photographic film. Most prominent of these things is the sky.

A deep-blue sky and fleecy clouds are valuable assets to any scenic picture, but in an ordinary snapshot it's quite likely the sky won't appear as dark or the clouds as fleecy as you'd expect them to be. All photographic films are especially sensitive to blue light and even more so to invisible ultraviolet radiation, both of which abound in the sky. To the film, then, the sky looks much nearer the brightness of the clouds than it looks to you.

There are dozens of filters which find some occupation in photography, but the most commonly used ones are those primarily designed to improve this sky-cloud deficiency. The yellow Kodak Pictorial Filter and the Kodak Cloud Filter produce pictures in which the relationship is about as it appears to the eye. With the red Pictorial Filter, skies become dramatically dark, trees and grass are darkened somewhat, and faces turn white. A green Pictorial Filter has about the same effect on the sky as the yellow one, but also produces lighter-colored foliage and particularly pleasant skin tones.

No filter, like no photographer, is perfect, and each kind will filter out not only the color of light it is manufactured to stop but also some light of all the other colors, too. This makes it necessary to increase the amount of exposure given the film when employing most filters. Such increases aren't possible on box cameras when the Kodak Cloud Filter is in use, but the exposure latitude of Kodak Verichrome Pan Film is sufficient to allow for the amount of light absorbed by the filter.

Filters for color films

Place a yellow Kodak filter over your camera lens when the film inside is color film and the filter's most pronounced contribution to your snapshots will be a sickly yellow pall which makes them look as if they were suffering from an advanced case of jaundice. Color films don't commonly need any filtering, and even when a filter will be beneficial, the ones used are an entirely different breed from the deepcolored monocles employed for black-and-white snapping.

Exhibit A is the Kodak Skylight Filter (Wratten No. 1A). The slight pink tint in this filter is so faint that it requires no extra camera exposure when in use. But this slight pinkness is sufficient to eradicate much of the characteristic blueness of pictures made on Daylight Type color films under cloudy or shaded conditions.

Exhibit B is a filter that hasn't any real color at all, the Kodak Pola-Screen. This talented piece of what looks like ordinary gray glass specializes in darkening skies and rubbing out glaring reflections without affecting any other colors in the picture. It will do this, however, only when the sun is at right angles to whatever you are snapping. If you rotate a Pola-Screen in front of your eye while looking out on any side-lighted scene, you'll see the appearance of the sky change from its normal blue to an extremely dark, dramatic, purplish-blue. This often contributes an extra measure of pictorial interest to color snapshots. When adjusted to provide the maximum polarizing effect, a Pola-Screen will necessitate a considerable increase in exposure. With Ektachrome-X Film, Daylight

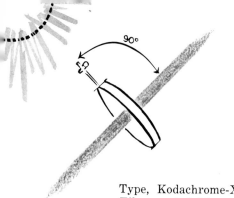

A Kodak Pola-Screen is effective only when a scene is lighted from the side or above. For maximum sky-darkening effect, the handle on its rim should be pointed toward the sun.

Type, Kodachrome-X, Daylight Type, and Kodacolor-X Film on a bright, sunny day, the basic setting is 1/60, f 8; with Kodachrome II, Daylight Type, the exposure in 1/60, f 5.6.

The Kodak Daylight Filter for Kodak Type B Color Films (Wratten No. 85B) lets you shoot High Speed Ektachrome Film, Type B, in daylight. Filtered Type B film requires one stop more exposure than High Speed Ektachrome, Daylight Type. This still leaves plenty of speed, though, and the Type B film-plus-filter combination is a good choice if you want to make all your color slides on a single, fast film.

Another widely employed filter for color films is the Kodak Daylight Filter for Kodak Type A Color Films (Wratten No. 85). This filter is primarily for movie films but can be used with Kodachrome II Professional Film, Type A, using the same lens opening as for Kodachrome II Daylight Type Film.

A horizon is only a straight line until you snap something evocative on it; a lighthouse may be pretty, but the gulls give it authentic flavor. Dark skies in both are from a yellow filter.

A suitable exposure for the twilight silhouette of the ferris wheel would be 1/25, ƒ 5.6 on Kodachrome II Film, Daylight Type; for the house, 1/60 at ƒ 8 with an early morning hazy sun.

Time exposures

A time exposure takes time. So does a cake. But a cake recipe will always specify so-many minutes and such-and-such temperature, while information on time exposures seems hopelessly vague in comparison. It's a happy fact, though, that while exact data for time exposures is almost impossible to list, there isn't any real need to be exact.

The only highly critical element in this sort of snapping is camera stability. Tremorless though they may be, your own hands become a highly unsatisfactory platform for a camera when the shutter time is much greater than 1/25 second. Whether you choose a tripod, a Kodak Flexiclamp, or some makeshift like a table, fence, or windowsill, there just can't be any wiggle or wobble during the exposure.

Time exposures are most applicable when there isn't sufficient light for an ordinary snapshot and when the subject is too massive to be illuminated by flash. This is just another way of saying late-twilight and night scenes. One important reason why time exposures are so easy to

Four bursts of pyrotechnics caught in one time exposure; the Christmas tree in Brooklyn required 5 seconds at *f* 16 with Kodak Tri-X Film.

make is that, with typical subjects, it's extremely difficult to overexpose your shots. Only extreme overexposure will actually ruin a picture.

An almost sure way of coming up with a satisfactory time snapshot is to try a trio of widely varying exposures. Lens settings for an adjustable camera might be *f* 5.6 with most color films and Kodak Panatomic-X Film, *f*/11 with Verichrome Pan and Plus-X Pan, and *f* 16 with Tri-X. For your first exposure, try one second; for the next, about five seconds; for the last, about thirty seconds. Except when the scene is very dimly lighted, one of these should yield a near-perfect result.

Kodak High Speed Ektachrome Film, Type B, is the exceptionally fast color film that lets you capture brightly-lit city streets after dark with hand-held snapshot speeds. Try 1/25 or 1/30 second at *f* 2 or *f* 2.8.

Adjustable cameras have a provision for making time exposures in the form of a setting marked "B" or "Bulb" or "Brief Time" or "Long" or "L." When you use it, the camera shutter will stay open as long as you press the button.

This arrangement is fine for fairly short time exposures but a finger tends to become restless and, after a while, may shift position just enough to jar the camera and spoil the picture. With a box camera, there's nothing much you can do about this except steel yourself or perhaps try yoga. With adjustable cameras, a cable release makes it easier to take time exposures without moving the camera.

Christmas is usually a wonderful time for time exposures, particularly if your home or some part of your neighborhood is decorated with lights. Color film, of course, will do the most exciting job here. Fireworks displays are another place for a variation on time-exposure technique. Merely point the camera toward the place where the fireworks will explode, open the shutter, wait for three or four bursts, and then close it. Another time-exposure location is the local amusement park. Try a fifteen-second shot of a moving ferris wheel or some other ride, and you should get a striking whirl of colored light.

Snapping at sunset

Sunsets in black-and-white are striking and handsome. Sunsets in color are breathtaking. And sunsets in color with a person or some recognizable object silhouetted against the sky are not only breathtaking but one of the most meaningful and telling kinds of scenic pictures anyone can take.

Sunset views largely suggest themselves. And exposure is no problem. With the sun still visible above the horizon, try settings of 1/50, *f* 6.3 with Kodachrome II; 1/100, *f* 8 with Kodak Ektachrome-X, Kodachrome-X, and Kodacolor-X; and 1/100 at *f* 11 with Kodak High Speed Ektachrome Film, Daylight Type. The Daylight Type materials accentuate the warm glowing hues of pictures made at sunset. A box-camera snapshot made with Kodacolor Film will probably be slightly underexposed, but the film has sufficient latitude to provide a colorful picture.

For black-and-white shooting, settings of 1/50, *f* 6.3 with a red filter over the lens should be about right for Kodak Verichrome Pan and Plus-X Pan Films. All of these exposure suggestions are fallible, and it's advisable to make a pair of insurance shots, one with the lens open three settings wider and one closed down three settings smaller.

Once the sun has drifted out of sight but left behind a bright afterlight, some good starting points for an exposure trio are 1/25, *f* 3.5 with Kodachrome II and Kodacolor; 1/60, *f* 3.5 with Kodachrome-X, Ektachrome-X, and Kodacolor-X; or 1/60, *f* 5.6 with Kodak High Speed Ektachrome Film.

The palette of sunset is stocked with stirring colors. Settings of 1/60, ƒ 11 for Kodachrome-X, Ektachrome-X and Kodacolor-X; and 1/60, ƒ 6.3 for Kodachrome II, and Kodacolor are good starting points when the sun is still visible, but in any sunset situation shoot several shots at different settings as insurance.

Snapshots of VACATION *and* TRAVEL

*The crowd waits, silent in expectancy.
Suddenly, with a subterranean
rumble, the first burst of steam and
water thrusts from the ground.
Its white column rises in fitful jerks
until, well over a hundred feet tall,
the crest plumes off into the wind.*

*The people relax now and shout to
each other over the hissing. For five
minutes the geyser spouts continuously
and then, its energy spent, the
cascade begins gradually to fall
and shrink. As it came, it goes.
The crowd pauses a moment,
then wanders slowly away.*

*You see this all from beside
your projector in the brief instant
a single slide is on the screen.
For a split second, this one part
of this one vacation
is vividly real again.*

A sorrowful case history with a moral

Mr. X (name withheld out of embarrassment) departed for his European vacation with a brand new little 35mm camera in one hand and two dozen 36-exposure rolls of Kodachrome Film in his luggage. Touring the continent, he carefully and purposefully exposed each picture to compile a thorough photographic chronicle of his travels. There was only one little thing wrong. This new camera shutter required manual cocking, something to which Mr. X wasn't accustomed, but which he could have discovered by checking the instructions. The shutter hadn't opened once. Mr. X, thorough in all matters but one, was out his pictures, the cost of his film, and the expense of processing it.

Tragedies like this can be averted easily and inexpensively through a two-part, pre-vacation safety program.

Part 1—A couple of weeks before leaving, snap a roll of black-and-white pictures and have them processed immediately. This will check your own proficiency and will tell you if anything has happened to your camera that might affect its operation.

Part 2—Then take the camera to your favorite camera shop and let their service department check it. This will tell you if anything is on the verge of happening.

But don't leave this for the very last minute. And follow the same procedure with your exposure meter, if you have one.

The care of color film

Color film is an almost automatic choice for vacation snapshooting, particularly if you plan to go touring. Only color pictures capture the high points of your vacation in such vividly memorable form. But how should film be purchased, protected, and processed when you are following a gypsy program?

The crux of this three-pronged teaser is that high humidity and high temperature are relentless foes of unprocessed color film.

The humidity menace is kept well under control, at least before you load the film in your camera, by Kodak's air-tight packaging. Heat damage can be prevented by merely keeping film out of obvious hot spots. A few of the worst ones in an automobile are the trunk, the glove compartment, and the deck behind the rear seat.

Whether you buy all of your film from your local dealer or pick it up along your route is entirely a matter of personal preference. Kodak color film is available in every part of the United States, even in many fairly remote vacation areas. But always be sure to carry a spare roll or two just for those circumstances when you encounter a breath-taking snapshot opportunity but the nearest source of film is twelve miles down the road.

Even if you decide against purchasing all of your color film from your local dealer, definitely make arrangements with him before leaving so that you can mail each roll back to him for processing. In this way you'll not only be likely to see your pictures sooner but will avoid possible complications and any damage to the film that might occur if you carried it with you for an extended period.

When to snap people and when to snap things

Have you ever been treated to a slide or snapshot showing accompanied by a narration sounding something like this?

"Yes, here's Martha at the Statue of Liberty and,
oh yes, here she is in Rockefeller Center, and
here's one of her in front of Grant's Tomb and . ."

Out of each snapshot smiles Martha's warm and friendly face, but all that's evident of these picture-worthy landmarks is a fringe of masonry and, perhaps, part of a torch-bearing arm.

Each of us harbors some tendency to do this sort of thing and it certainly provides indisputable evidence of "I was there." Succumbing once in a while won't cause the sky to fall, but try to keep it from becoming habitual. To put it bluntly, Martha will still be with you when you get back home, but, other than photographically, you can't bring Grant's Tomb along without incurring the hostility of the New York City Police Department.

For the greatest mileage from your color-film investment, discipline yourself to shoot scenery as scenery and to shoot the members of your vacation party doing the kinds of things they either couldn't do around home or that are characteristic of the places being visited. On a camping trip, snap them pitching the tent, chopping wood, fishing, plunging in for a late-afternoon swim. If your pleasure is sight-seeing, catch them walking down picturesque streets or buying souvenirs.

WASHINGTON, D.C.

The earlier you get up in Washington, the better. Late risers miss the beauty of landmarks outlined against the sunrise sky. But at any time of day you can climb the Washington Monument for a

Brothers' first airplane, the Declaration of Independence, many halls of historic statuary, and the masterpieces of the National Gallery. In late afternoon, the giant Marine Corps Memorial is a

view of the Lincoln Memorial or admire the golden equestrian statues at the approach to the Arlington Bridge. Indoors, Washington is a vast museum housing such treasures as the Wright

straining silhouette against a still-blue sky and, as night falls, the Capitol dome, the National Archives, and other government buildings gleam against the darkness in their aura of floodlights.

When your family embarks on a vacation trip, shoot both what you *do* and what you *see*. For the best pictures of scenery, pose people in the foreground but make sure they're looking at the attraction, not at the camera. And don't forget important sign-posts with, perhaps, someone in your group reading them.

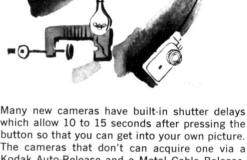

Many new cameras have built-in shutter delays which allow 10 to 15 seconds after pressing the button so that you can get into your own picture. The cameras that don't can acquire one via a Kodak Auto-Release and a Metal Cable Release. To complete your self-snapping kit, add a Kodak Flexiclamp for a compact, inexpensive means of mounting the camera firmly.

Snapshooting abroad

When you depart from the United States, many things change abruptly, but none of them affect the motions you go through in snapping a picture. You still use the same basic exposure settings, still squeeze the same button, still advance the film after each exposure.

The differences you'll encounter will be differences in supplying yourself with photographic materials and arranging to have your film processed. Customs regulations covering the amount of film you may carry duty free from one country to another aren't entirely uniform, and individual customs officers sometimes use considerable discretion in interpreting them. A friendly, co-operative attitude on your part in your relations with customs authorities can often move mountains.

Here are a few basic considerations that may influence the photographic logistics for any trip you plan:

All film, but particularly color film, should be processed as soon as possible after exposure and shouldn't be carried home with you in your luggage unprocessed unless your trip is an extremely brief one.

SCANDINAVIA

The sea is the great highway of Northern Europe, and across its waters the Northmen sailed to their epics of conquest and discovery. The lives of present-day Scandinavians are tied almost as closely to the oceans as those of their antecedents. All the great

chase fresh fish, crocheted shopping sacks, real flowers, or brightly colored artificial flowers made from feathers glued to twigs. Street parades are a great attraction, and Norwegian children appreciate a good vantage point as much as any other

cities, like Stockholm here, are seaports. Many of their most handsome, historical buildings stand at harbor's edge, overlooking the procession of ships from all over the world. In these cities, great plazas are used as open-air markets in which you can pur-

children. Artistically, Scandinavians have made their most outstanding achievements in sculpture, and Oslo's Frogner Park has a marvelous tableau by Vigeland of life-size, lifelike stone figures depicting the common experience and struggle of mankind.

You'll probably be moving around pretty rapidly and this, combined with the unpredictable length of time necessary for color film processing, makes it inadvisable to plan on having film returned to you abroad unless you allow an extremely generous safety factor.

All Kodak film, particularly color film, is more expensive outside the United States.

Black-and-white film in most popular sizes is readily obtainable almost everywhere and can usually be satisfactorily processed in most cities, often with 24-hour delivery; hotel personnel can usually advise you which photo-finishing establishments offer such service.

Kodacolor Film is now sold in all the principal countries or marketing areas throughout the world. Make certain, however, that if you have your Kodacolor Film processed by some color photofinisher on the Continent, you make adequate arrangements for its return to you at some stop on your itinerary or at your home in this country.

Kodachrome and Kodak Ektachrome Film are available nearly everywhere in the world. There are Kodak Processing Laboratories in many countries for the processing of both films, but they cannot return slides to your U.S. address without special arrangements.

"Planning and Taking Your Travel Pictures" contains helpful data for travelers. The price is 75 cents at your Kodak dealer's.

When you're up in the air, literally

Any camera thrives on altitude, and even unpretentious little box cameras can make first-rate aerial shots. A perch aloft presents an unsurpassed opportunity for pictures of really king-size attractions, such as distinctive cities, mountains, rivers, and other topographical wonders.

It's easiest to make good snapshots when the plane has reached an altitude of at least 2000 feet, since the ground then doesn't move by so rapidly. The best snap-shooting seats in a commercial airliner are aft of the wing and on the side away from the direct rays of the sun. On an eastbound flight, try to sit on the left side; on a westbound flight, the right side.

All planes vibrate, and for sharp photographic results make certain your arms aren't resting against the seat or any other structural part of the aircraft. The camera should be close to the window but not touching it.

Old reliable Kodak Verichrome Pan Film is tops for box-camera black-and-white aerial snapping. It will do a mighty good job unassisted but an even better one with a Kodak Cloud Filter over the lens to wipe out some of the light haze that may be in the air. For color shots, Kodacolor Film and sunlight are an unbeatable team.

When making black-and-white pictures with an adjustable camera, it's advisable to employ an equivalent exposure for the sunlight conditions that gives you a shutter time of 1/200 second. This not only tends to tame the vibration of the plane but also the effect of the plane's forward motion. Black-and-white films are peculiarly sensitive to the blue haze that usually permeates the air, and this haze will often be more evident in a snapshot than it is to the eye. To counteract it, do your black-and-white shooting through a yellow filter. Above 4000 feet and with this filter over the lens, your exposure settings are exactly what they'd be at ground level without the filter. On a bright, sunny day, and with Verichrome Pan Film in your camera, an exposure of 1/200, *f* 11 will do the trick; for Panatomic-X Film, use settings of 1/200, *f* 5.6 with a yellow filter. Below 4000 feet, try a lens opening half-way toward the next *wider* setting.

With Kodak color slide films, Daylight Type, much of the haze problem can be tamed by a Kodak Skylight Filter over the lens. This filter isn't necessary for Kodacolor Film. Exposure settings for above 4000 feet, with or without the Skylight Filter, are 1/200 *f* 5.6 for Kodachrome II, Ektachrome, and Kodacolor; and 1/200, *f* 22, for High Speed Ektachrome.

95

Good aerial views communicate a wondrous grandeur. The clouds in this one, even though they obscure much of the ground, create a better shot than you'd get on a clear day.

Snapshots of FLOWERS

and other

SMALL

OBJECTS

Thumbs come not only in an extensive variety of sizes but in all colors, too. Twice blessed, though, is he whose initial digit is green, for he has a communion with the soil that is akin to magic. Not only is he able to raise blooms of surpassing size and shape, but with almost any camera he can preserve their glory in close-up color snapshots.

If you are among the chosen few or even a mere digger-and-hoper, the next seven pages should reveal a wonderful world of photographic pleasure.

But everyone doesn't like flowers. Reaction to them can vary from casual apathy to the open enmity of a rose-fever sufferer who feels his sinuses twitch at the mere sight of a nursery catalogue.

But if not a bud man, you may be a bug man, and the techniques for snapping a delphinium will apply equally well to a dragonfly. And if neither buds nor bugs are your personal pot of tea, perhaps birds' eggs, home-polished gems, or scale-model railroad equipment you've painstakingly tweezered together will provide the necessary inspiration to make these pages breathtakingly interesting.

If not, the pictures are pretty and there's a fascinating section on shooting action snapshots immediately beyond.

Equipment for ultra close-ups

There's no statute against bringing the lens of your trusty old box camera right up to the nose of a bee for a breathtaking close-up, but you're likely to be stung in more ways than one. First, the bee may resent the intrusion on his privacy, and second, the shot will be irrecognizably fuzzy.

Sharpness is vital. For box cameras, the closest distance practical for a sharp picture with a Kodak Close-up Attachment is $3\frac{1}{2}$ feet; they can be used, however, at 32 inches, 18 inches, and 12 inches, respectively, with a 1+, 2+, and 3+ Kodak Portra Lens.

Adjustable cameras can fire away from as close as about $5\frac{1}{2}$ inches by means of only a pair of Portra Lenses in front of the regular lens, and some precision cameras will make sharp shots even closer with the aid of a bellows housing something like the one on a studio camera or with other highly specialized equipment.

Kodak Portra Lenses 1+, 2+, and 3+, either individually or in combination, provide a simple and inexpensive system for snapping an individual blossom or some other miniature. They have the effect of radically changing the range of distances over which a camera is capable of making a sharp picture. A lens that will focus sharply between four feet and infinity is capable of focusing on objects between $21\frac{1}{2}$ and 39 inches away when a 1+ Portra Lens is mounted over it. The ranges of these lenses and combinations are:

Kodak Portra Lens	Focusing Range
1+	$21\frac{1}{2}$ to 39 inches
2+	14 to $19\frac{1}{2}$ inches
3+	$10\frac{1}{2}$ to 13 inches
3+ and 1+	$8\frac{1}{4}$ to 10 inches
3+ and 2+	7 to 8 inches
3+ and 3+	$5\frac{1}{2}$ to $6\frac{1}{2}$ inches

With a 3+ Portra Lens used at its nearest distance, your camera will cover an area about 5 by 7 inches, making it ideal for the great majority of garden subjects and most other small objects. For comparison, a pair of 3+ Portra Lenses permits a camera to take in a rectangle about 3 by $4\frac{1}{2}$ inches. A complete table of areas covered by Portra Lenses is included in the Kodak Master Photoguide, a pocket-size compendium of photo data which also features several handy computing dials.

Using Portra Lenses

In Portra Lens territory, the range of sharpness is hardly worth calling a range at all. There just plain isn't enough of it to be worth talking about. Since this wipes out any margin of error, it's essential to take an actual measurement before each shot. The measurement, by the way, should cover the distance from the front surface of the Portra Lens to the front of the subject.

A convenient way to avoid computations is by attaching a string to your camera with one knot at the closest shooting distance possible and one at the farthest. These are obtained by consulting a table packed with each Portra Lens. If you confine your shooting to one or the other of the two distances, using the knots as measuring guides, you need never resort to a yardstick.

A steady camera is equally as vital as a well-focused one. When snapping by sunshine, employ a shutter time of 1/25 second and take extra pains to avoid camera movement. If the day is breezy, however, you'd better shift to 1/50 second. In flash shots, this is much less of a problem, since the very popular No. 5 and 25 lamps provide nearly all of their illumination in 1/50 second, and most of the other widely used lamps are even briefer in their performance, thus giving you the benefits of a brief shutter time.

10½ inches   13 inches

With a Portra Lens 3+, you might attach to your camera a string with a knot tied at the correct shooting distance when the camera lens is focused at infinity and another at the distance when it is focused at, let's say, four feet. You can then eliminate considerable calculation by doing all your shooting at one or the other of these two distances.

Portra Lenses will transform small objects of nature into massive proportions, exposing a world of color entirely unnoticed at normal viewing distances.

A phenomenon called "parallax" and how to lick it

Most cameras have two glass "eyes," one through which you look at a picture and the other through which the film does. In most photographic situations this bright but rather obvious little trinket of information carries about the same practical significance as the grazing habits of the beast that supplied your camera's leather covering.

However, when any camera approaches near enough to a subject so that a Portra Lens becomes indispensable, this changes abruptly. At close range, the viewfinder obtains a different view of the subject than the camera lens, and the closer the range, the more different this becomes.

With a single Portra Lens, either $1+$, $2+$, or $3+$, there's a comparatively uncomplicated solution. It's merely a matter of arranging the picture in your viewfinder as you ordinarily would and then, just before you snap, shifting its position slightly to compensate for the spacing between viewfinder lens and picture-taking lens. If the camera is in horizontal position, tip it up by about 1/4 of the picture area as you see it in the finder for a $3+$ lens, 1/6 for a $2+$, and 1/8 for a $1+$. When employing a vertical format, use the same fractions and do the tipping toward the finder.

Closer-up than the operating range of a $3+$ Portra Lens, the viewfinder on all except single-lens reflex cameras becomes almost useless. For shooting of this sort, it's essential that you have attached to your camera a piece of hardware which not only indicates the distance at which picture subjects should be from the camera for a particular combination of Portra Lenses but also marks off the exact area covered. Such hardware items are called "focal frames" and may either be purchased from a camera dealer or fashioned at home from a length of iron rod, a block of wood, and a few screws.

The most painless, accurate, civilized way of all to make close-up pictures is with a single-lens reflex camera. Such cameras have no separate viewfinder window for you to look through. When you peer through the viewfinder, you're actually looking right out through the lens that takes the pictures. Your eye sees exactly what the film will see, with any lens, at any distance. The beauty of this arrangement for close-up pictures is that you can *see* whether the picture will be sharp and properly framed, right through the viewfinder. There's no need to use focal frames or measuring devices, and no problem of parallax. Whatever you see, you get. The Kodak Retina Reflex S Camera is an example of such a talented picturetaker.

A word on backgrounds

There's a wonderful ego-priming feature to ultra close-up photography. It's that if you handle adroitly the mechanical factors, such as exposure, framing, focus, and camera steadiness, the æsthetic end of things just seems to take care of itself.

Perhaps, with a Kodak Portra Lens mounted on your camera, you're snapping a single flower in its natural habitat. Simplicity of arrangement and approach are, of course, the hallmarks of any really attractive flower picture. Well, if you do your shooting by flash, the blossom will appear isolated against a plain black background, since nothing behind it will be sufficiently illuminated to register on the film; by sunlight, the background, although visible, is so extremely out of focus that it becomes a pleasant, hazy, unobtrusive curtain of color that complements the subject without distracting attention from it.

In some cases, particularly when photographing scale models, choice of a background is entirely in your own hands. For a rainbow selection at a penny-wise price, the large sheets of dull-finish colored paper available from art supply stores are ideal. With such objects as toy soldiers, you can place them on one end of the sheet while raising the other end about a foot and fastening it there so that it forms both flat surface and backdrop. When your target is the bloom of a potted plant or some other part of a larger whole, the paper can simply be attached to a wall about a foot or two behind the subject.

For color shots, it's usually advisable to select a fairly flat, rather than bright, background shade that will contrast with the color of the subject. In black-and-white shooting, a light-gray background is best for dark subjects; a fairly dark or black one, for light subjects. These, like all generalized semi-rules, are often broken with handsome effect and it certainly does no harm to experiment.

To picture clusters of bright flowers like these dwarf marigolds, the Portra Lens can be removed, and the camera focused for some regular close-up distance, say, three feet.

Small pets or wildlife are not only interesting to snap close-up but rather challenging. It's essential to handle your focal-frame equipment slowly and gently so as not to alarm them.

Even such seemingly unlovely floral specimens as the dried blossom of the salsify, an herb, reveal unsuspected order and beauty when examined by a Kodak Portra Lens at 7½ inches.

A fern fastened directly behind a flower contributes not only its own attractive pattern but a feeling of woodland authenticity. It is particularly attractive when the flower is of a delicate hue.

105

Snapshots of
SPECIAL EVENTS

"Ugh, I hate picnics—all ants and sand in the food,"
sourly states a poor, put-upon soul, but once there
he's the fellow who organizes the three-legged race,
does the whale imitation in the lake, and attempts
to devour a quarter of a watermelon solo.
"Me, preside at a kids' party with that mob of
juvenile delinquents? No thanks." But an hour later
this misanthrope is elbowing small fry out of the way
to bob for apples or is off in the living room
demonstrating the Charleston.
People are like this. You can be certain
the very girl who sneers most loudly that
weddings are just means of legalizing feminine
slavery will always be the first to sniffle happily
during the ceremony. And, those of us who are
dragged protesting to these special events
somehow are the ones who remonstrate most bitterly
if no one bothers to take snapshots or if the number
of snapshots is scant, or particularly, if we aren't
amply represented in the photographic coverage.
These occasions are the delightful, memorable
threads that bind together the often featureless

fabric of our daily lives. So even if you, yourself,
may attend some of them over your own objections,
take along a camera and some film just in case
you suddenly find yourself having a good time.

Long after the last choruses of "Happy Birthday" have died away, even after the gifts are worn out or discarded, a party can remain as real as ice cream and cake through color photographs. The pictures of a child's party should tell a story with a beginning (like giving a crinoline a last minute hitch) and an ending (savoring a particularly appreciated present), in addition to the more traditional high points. These snapshots were made on Kodachrome Film, Daylight Type, by the bright sunlight filtering into a screened porch.

At parties

If a photographer from a major picture magazine covered a party, either adult or juvenile, at your home, here's how he'd probably handle it.

First, he'd do a thorough job of shooting the party preparations—setting up of decorations, production of edibles, dressing for the occasion.

Then he'd snap pictures of the guests arriving. At a costume party he'd make at least one shot of everyone. If it was an occasion that called for gifts, especially gifts for a child, he'd try to capture the excitement of opening them.

He'd concentrate on the action of the party but in a special way. He'd try to remain as inconspicuous as possible. He'd allow activities, particularly games, to get well under way before he'd move in close with his camera and begin snapping. Chances are that he'd wait at least a few minutes between shots so that the participants would have time to forget that someone was taking pictures.

At the end, he wouldn't forget to make some snapshots of the departing guests. Probably, too, he'd snap the host or hostess surveying the post-party scene.

And what *he* would do, *you* can do also.

An outdoor party, as you might guess, is the easiest kind to photograph. Outdoors a camera is less of a distracting influence and this contributes to better, more natural results.

Indoors, as usual, flash is the first source of lighting that comes to mind. Owners of adjustable cameras, how-

110

On sunny days, enough light filters into most rooms so that entire parties can be photographed without flash. Even though the window shades were pulled down, it was possible to expose this picture at settings of 1/50 *f* 2.8 on Kodak Tri-X Film.

ever, have two other interesting options. In a well-lighted room, pictures can be made without flash by putting Kodak Tri-X Pan Film to work. There may well be enough light to make color pictures on Kodak High Speed Ektachrome Film. There's a section on this technique which begins on page 149.

The other possibility for black-and-white snapping with adjustable cameras is a method called bounce flash. The idea, here, is one of directing the light from a flash lamp toward a ceiling so that it bounces off and fills the entire room. It is described in detail in the section beginning on page 144.

For bounce-lighted snapping at a party, the best approach is to clamp a flash holder to the back of a chair in one corner of the room. A Kodak Flexiclamp will take care of this nicely. Then connect the flash holder to your camera with a flash extension cord. This cord may be anywhere from 3 to 20 feet in length and allows freedom to move around in an average size room and snap pictures. As long as the ceilings and walls are white or fairly light colored, bounce flash can be counted upon to provide fine snapshots with a minimum of interference in the party, itself.

Party activities are certainly the chief excuse for having a camera around on festive occasions, but there are often many pre-party sidelights worthy of an exposure or two. Witness the sampling of the baker's art being made at right.

To capture both the picnickers and campfire, proceed as if you were snapping an ordinary flash shot at a shutter time of 1/25. Actually, though, set the shutter on "B" or "L" and keep the button pressed down for a couple of seconds after the lamp has fired.

On picnics

Whether a picnic is a small, family affair or draws a crowd in the hundreds, it inevitably begins at home. For a complete photo log of the day, start around the house with some snapshots of food preparation, car loading, and other preliminaries. If you are shooting your pictures in color, you'll find Kodacolor Film ideal in these circumstances since, on the same roll of film, it permits you to snap indoors with clear flash lamps and outdoors by sunlight.

You can obtain the same sort of convenience with Kodak color slide films, Daylight Type. For outdoor shots by daylight, merely do your snapping as you ordinarily would. For indoor shots by flash, you can either use a filter on the camera lens for clear flash bulbs, or you can use blue bulbs without a filter. The filter you need is the Kodak Photoflash

Filter No. 80C plus an adapter ring to hold it over your camera's lens mount. Unless you're doing a lot of flash photography, you may prefer blue bulbs. The film instruction sheets give flash-exposure guide numbers to work out camera settings.

A good outing is something more than a group of people gawking self-consciously at a camera, so try to make your pictures show more of the picnic than this. It isn't necessary to let your camera take you to the picnic, but try to steal a few moments every once in a while to snap whatever is going on.

It's also a good idea to pack your flash holder and bring a few flash lamps along. With color film, your most memorable shot can easily be one made around the fire after dark. There's a special trick to shooting this since, if you followed customary flash procedure, there'd be no evidence of the fire in your picture. It's an old photographic maxim that you can't shoot light with light.

With a box camera, set the shutter on "L" and follow the distances you use for ordinary flash snapping; with an adjustable camera, choose your lens opening on the basis of the recommendations given for 1/25 second but set the shutter on "B." After the flash lamp has fired, keep the button pressed down while you say to yourself, "One-thousand-and-one." Then release it.

Ordinarily, a camera shouldn't be handheld for exposures longer than 1/25 second. In this case, the flash discharges all its light in 1/50 second or less. This provides a sharp picture of the people but no picture of the fire. The remainder of the exposure allows the fire to register. Even if your camera should be slightly unsteady after the flash, there won't be enough light from the fire to disturb the images of the people. The fire, itself, will not turn out sharply, but there is no means by which this could be achieved anyway.

113

Let five boys loose around a fireplace and, before you can rub two sticks together, you'll have the raw material for a terrific bunch of snapshots.

A wedding really begins at the moment a bride tries on her veil and, for the first time, sees herself as a bride. It's a wondrous instant, one you can capture without fuss or flash on Tri-X Film.

At weddings

It takes only two to make a marriage but a great deal more to make a wedding; something every bride's father discovers sooner or later. One prime ingredient is pictures. At many weddings these days, a professional photographer is commissioned to compile a bridal photo log, but even when this is the case there's still plenty of opportunity for snapshooting. A "pro" is only one man with one head and he can't possibly be everywhere at once. Also, you'll find that the wedding party, its family and friends, have an insatiable appetite for snapshots and more snapshots.

To shoot a complete wedding story you would have to begin at the rehearsal or even at some of the activities that precede it. Then, early on the chosen day, you'd snap many of the important preparations made by the bride and groom. Next, you'd get pictures of both participants arriving at the appointed place, shoot as many as possible during the ceremony, cover the reception, and wind up with the getaway of the newly married couple.

This, of course, is a demanding schedule but your results will be their own reward.

To do any snapping during the actual ceremony, good manners dictate that you request permission of the bride, groom, and the person performing it. The use of flash is definitely out. Weddings are too solemn occasions to be punctuated with the sporadic bursts of light from flash lamps. Unfortunately, when you eliminate flash lamps you also eliminate box cameras. Actually, the situation isn't entirely dismal for the box camera-ite since the procession after the ceremony and the activities along the receiving line can be flash snapped without violating etiquette.

An adjustable camera loaded with Kodak Tri-X Film makes it possible to shoot wedding pictures in nearly any location without flash. Although churches and synagogues vary widely in lighting, exposure settings of 1/25, f/3.5 should be satisfactory in most of them when the weather is bright and sunny outdoors. If you'd like to have the freedom to move around a little for picture taking purposes during the ceremony, again be sure to ask permission. When granted, don't violate the privilege and don't get in the way of any professional photographer who may be at work. Be as discreet and quiet and unobtrusive as you possibly can.

For more complete data on use of Tri-X Film in existing light, read the section beginning on page 149.

The before-and-after of beautifying a bride-to-be are an integral part of the wedding story and easily snapped by anyone who goes along with her. In most fairly-well-lighted shops, you'd be able to get good results with settings of 1/50, f/2.8 on Tri-X Film.

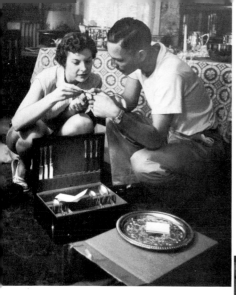

Although most families involved in the tumult of a wedding hire a professional photographer, many of the most memorable preparations occur hours or days before he'd be likely to appear on the scene. Kodak Tri-X Film captured most of these shots by the existing light. Only those made indoors at night required flash.

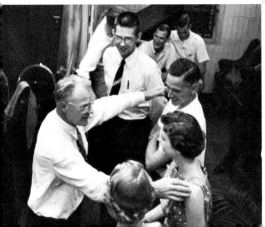

In an adjustable camera, Kodak Tri-X Pan Film will do as superlative a job outdoors after a wedding as it will indoors during the ceremony. On a bright day, settings of 1/25, $f/3.5$ will perform quite nicely in churches and synagogues having large windows. Outdoors, in bright sunlight, the basic exposure is 1/200, $f/22$. Be sure, though, to avoid interfering with any professional photographer on the job. His work, since it's being paid for, comes first.

119

Snapshots of

All sports activities involve a substantial element of lunacy. What else would induce people to spend long summer hours zig-zagging across closely-clipped pastures in an attempt to insert a small ball into a small hole with entirely inadequate implements. The entire history of games is marked with madness. Lacrosse was originally played by the male contingents of two entire Indian tribes with attendant casualties of a quantity and quality to compare favorably with the doings at Little Big Horn.

Even if your own exertions are restricted to such relatively sensible diversions as swatting a feathered ball with an undersized snowshoe or playing dismounted polo over a course marked by wire arches, they offer a release from the oppressive sanity that infects the greater part of our daily life. So swing stoutly, let the rules fall where they may, and don't forget a snapshot or two to record your athletics for later perusal under the grim and sober light of reason.

SPORTS *and* ACTION

Ideas especially for box camera action snapping

Most sports involve motion. Some of them, like fishing, are largely sedentary but their most memorable moments are likely to be charged with action. A color close-up of a trout fisherman with his fly-dotted hat and high-waisted waders will be a pleasant addition to any snapshot collection but neither you nor he will value it nearly as much as a picture of him actually struggling to net a speckled beauty.

Box cameras and, indeed, any cameras set at the box camera shutter time, 1/50 second, have definite drawbacks for snapping sports action. Most sports subjects move enough in 1/50 second to cause some blurring in a picture.

One way *not* to lick this is by pressing the exposure button on your camera very fast and hard. No matter how swiftly this button is punched, the shutter time will still be 1/50 second. Since punching doesn't reduce the shutter time but does increase chances of jarring the entire camera, make certain always to squeeze the button gently.

An important semi-solution to the shutter time limitation imposed by a box camera is to station yourself so that any action will come directly toward you. This minimizes

Action can be shot with a box camera by panning (notice blurred fence in left photo) and having subjects move toward you.

the effect of the motion and often makes it possible to shoot successfully subjects that would come out a featureless blob from any other angle. Many action shots taken in this manner have areas which are slightly blurred but this often makes them better pictures than they would have been if everything was perfectly frozen.

Another, but a more difficult solution, is snapping during periods of what might be called "suspended action." The final instant of a punter's follow-through, the top of a golfer's backswing, the pole vaulter's release of his pole—these are all moments during which there is little, if any, true motion. Unfortunately, though, they are extremely brief moments and the actual snapping must be timed perfectly.

There's one other widely used trick for box camera action snapping and it's a trick that violates one of the most oft cited principles in this book. On about every second or third page we have some kind of caution about holding your camera perfectly steady when you snap. For shooting certain moving subjects, things like cars, boats, and planes, there is a technique called "panning" in which camera movement is the key to success.

As a subject of this sort approaches, center it in your camera viewfinder. Then keep moving the camera along with the subject so that it stays centered in the finder. Whenever you wish, just snap. Your snapshot will show the car or boat or plane perfectly sharp while the background, due to the camera motion, will be blurred. This blurring should be of no objection since the background is probably of little importance and the blurring emphasizes the feeling of speed.

Panning, unhappily, doesn't apply too well for snapping fast-moving people or animals since their motion is not uniformly in one direction.

Which shutter time?

The tantalizing selection of action-stopping shutter times on most adjustable cameras can evoke responses that stray from the eenie-meenie-minie-mo system to a scientific approach which takes into consideration such elements as the speed of the subject in miles-per-hour, the direction of movement, the temperature, humidity, wind, time of day, and average annual rainfall. While some variation of this latter method may provide an accurate estimate of the necessary shutter time, it probably won't be a very practical one. By the time all your mathematical calculations are completed and checked, the subject will have gone that-a-way.

It's much handier to use an easily-remembered rule-of-thumb based on a trio of vital action-snapping principles:

1. A subject coming toward the camera shows less apparent movement than one moving at a 45° angle and one at a 45° angle shows less movement than one moving cross-ways.
2. The farther a subject is from the camera, the less apparent any movement will be.
3. It's always safer to use a shutter time that may be a little too brief than one that may be a bit too long.

The last thought suggests that it may be desirable to do all of your picture taking of sports activities with your camera set at the briefest shutter time of which it is capable. This is an easy solution and, generally, a good one. Its lone limitation is that as you shorten shutter time you must compensate by employing a larger lens opening and the wider the lens opening, the narrower the range of sharp focus.

Let's say, for example, that the basic exposure for the film in your camera and the lighting conditions is 1/100, *f* 16. If the quickest shutter time on your camera is 1/400

124

A boat sailing directly down on you might be snapped at a shutter time of 1/50 or with a box camera; sideways actions, however, require a setting of 1/200.

The volleyball picture is full of actual movement and demanded a brief shutter time. The basketball shot suggests motion even though none is really taking place. It was made without flash on Kodak Tri-X Film at exposure settings of 1/50, *f* 4.5.

and you wish to use it, the lens opening must be changed to one four times as wide or *f* 8. At *f* 8 the range of sharp focus is about half as wide as at *f* 16.

A lens opening of *f* 8 still permits quite a bit of focusing freedom. It's only when the resulting lens opening becomes *f* 3.5, *f* 2.8, or something of that order that this scheme begins to pinch a bit. As a rule you can feel safe in applying maximum shutter speed with Verichrome Pan Film and High Speed Ektachrome Film under all normal daylight conditions except deep shade; with Kodacolor, Ektachrome and Panatomic-X Films it works best for pictures taken by sunlight, either bright or hazy; with Kodachrome it becomes chancy except under bright sun.

The alternative would be to depend upon 1/200 or 1/300 for all but the very fastest sports or around-the-house action. Chances are good that it will satisfy nearly all your requirements. You can shift to 1/400, 1/500, or 1/800 if you have them available when you know the action will be extremely rapid or you must shoot it from the side or you

125

have to get in very close. When you don't have these extremely brief shutter times at your disposal, merely avoid tight close-ups and try to keep the movement coming toward your camera.

Shooting sports

Let's face facts. At major sporting events an amateur snap-shooter just cannot work his way down where the press photographers operate. Promoters of these events nurture a deep distaste for people who try to pass themselves off as professional lensmen and anyone who essays this gambit risks an abrupt bum's rush.

Fact number two. A grandstand seat almost always places you too far away from the action to shoot the kind of pictures that make the pages of newspapers and picture

It required a shutter time of 1/400 to freeze the fish, the rod, and the water. In a box-camera shot, they'd be blurred, although the angler's face might be sharp.

A shutter time of at least 1/200 is a must for anything that's thrown, whether a baby or a ball.

On a very dark day, an M5 or M25 flash lamp can help "stop" motion like this, even with a box-camera.

126

magazines. It's pretty much a waste of film even to try.

But you can get some fine snapshots of the overall scene from up in the stands and capture much of the atmosphere and excitement. At a big football game you can shoot the band formations, any card stunts, and the brightly uniformed teams lined up for scrimmage.

In a really well-lighted stadium you can probably make fine pictures at night if you have an adjustable camera. Although illumination standards vary from one stadium to another, a good starting point with Kodak Tri-X Film would be 1/50, $f/4$.

At more informal sports contests like Little League baseball games, Pee-Wee football struggles, and family croquet wars, a press card carries with it no special magic and snapshooters are more than welcome.

For snapping fast and/or sideways action on a dark day, try Kodak Tri-X Film. It permits you to use a brief shutter time without necessitating wide, shallow-focus lens openings.

This would hardly qualify as a sports shot, even though it may take a pretty good sport of a subject to appreciate it. While slightly fuzzy, it demonstrates pretty well what a box camera can do when the motion isn't too rapid.

127

Snapshot TRICKERY

Does the man really have an arrow in his chest?
Some people, you know, just haven't any idea when
to stop in a practical joke.

The fabled prankster, Wilson Mizener, never had
himself perforated with an arrow, but he did once
meet a midget with prodigiously large feet.
Sensing a brilliant opportunity, he hired him to
prop them on the windowsill of a hotel room
overlooking the Atlantic City boardwalk. When
Mizener and a friend "happened" along during a stroll
and noticed this unusual display, they launched into
a debate as to whether the size of a man's feet
could be used as an accurate indication of his height.
Mizener, of course, argued the negative. A sporting
wager resulted which enabled Mizener not only to
cover expenses but to enjoy a good chuckle
in the bargain.

According to the record, Mizener never employed
photography in his comic creations, but anyone
with the same sort of imagination and inclinations
will find it a valuable tool. The ideas
on the next two pages merely suggest the
potentialities and may be fairly tame compared
to those a really creative mind can conjure up.

And, by the way, while it's pretty certain
that the arrow isn't embedded in raw flesh,
we haven't yet doped out the how, why, and wherefore.

Trio?

Yes, it's just one young man, but he has not only a split personality but a split identity as well. Anyone, however, can be a trio, a quartet, or even quintuplets by virtue of some simple manipulation of the camera.

All that's involved is placing it on a tripod and shooting three (or even more, if you're ambitious) separate exposures on the same film. Between shots, your subject can change position and expression to suit the theme.

Best results are achieved indoors with a fairly distant, dark background. Any background will receive several times more exposure than the subject does in each position he takes, and the combination of distance and dark color will prevent it from becoming overexposed. Every exposure can be treated just as if it were a normal snapshot, but stationary props, especially ones in front of the subject, should be eliminated or minimized since they, too, are likely to be overexposed.

Balancing act

These gobs, despite appearances, would never interest Ringling Brothers, Barnum, and Bailey except as potential spectators. The upper one is definitely not a talented midget, and the lower one no demon at either feats of strength or balance.

All that's involved in making this kind of shot is lining things up carefully in your viewfinder (allow just a tiny gap between hand and foot to compensate for the slight difference in position of the camera lens and viewfinder lens) and making certain that both figures will be in sharp focus. With a box camera, it's necessary only to be sure that the nearest figure is at least five feet away; with an adjustable type, focus at some distance about halfway between your two performers and use the basic exposure given on the film instruction sheet, since it generally includes a small lens opening, and small lens openings provide a wide range of sharp focus.

131

Ghosts

Want a picture haunted? Again, the means is a double exposure. Again, a black background is helpful. Again, the camera should be on a tripod.

Arrange the picture area in your viewfinder and then set the camera so that the exposure will be just about one quarter of what you'd need for a normal snapshot. With a box camera, this means covering the flash holder with two or three thicknesses of white handkerchief; with an adjustable camera, it means using a lens opening two settings smaller than the one you'd normally employ.

Then shoot a picture of the "horror struck" subject and the "ghost" together. Make sure that the subject freezes in his position. Remove the "ghost" and shoot a second exposure in the same manner you'd employ for an ordinary flash snapshot.

132

Paste-up

This is a scissors-and-paste job, but one that must be handled with great delicacy and finesse. The idea, of course, is to cut out a photograph of a figure or figures and paste it down on another picture in some unlikely situation or pose. The final step is having your paste-up copied and prints made from the copy negative.

While small nail scissors can often do a pretty good job of figure silhouetting, a sharp hobby knife will probably provide more professional-looking results. To eliminate any sign of white edges around the cut-out, use a soft pencil to provide a less noticeable gray. Rubber cement is an ideal adhesive since it allows you to shift the position of the figure if your initial placement isn't quite right.

The unlikely human fly agility of the young man promenading down the sheer building wall is acquired from a scissors and paste pot. Note that even his shadow was kept from the original snapshot so as to create the greatest illusion of reality. The table-top fishing scene was created in identical manner. Since the fisherman's rod and line were too thin to cut out, they were sketched in with pen and ink on the paste-up before it was copied.

Flash-lamp characteristics and differences

A flash bulb is a happy combination of glass, gasses, lacquer, and metal that lets you make pictures of all the wonderful things that happen in your home—Thanksgiving dinners, parties, new babies in their cribs, the family around the Christmas tree, and the whole range of events that make life pleasant. Before we talk about flash pictures *per se,* let's examine the flash bulbs themselves.

Flash bulbs come in assorted shapes and sizes. They differ in such important respects as the amount of light they produce; the time required to reach peak light output; color; and cost.

To the uninitiated, the flash bulb situation can seem horribly complicated. Some bulbs that look alike aren't alike at all in terms of their photographic characteristics. The M2, M3, and M5 bulbs, for example, are three lookalikes that are quite different in light output and in time required to reach peak output. Some bulbs can be used at all shutter speeds on certain cameras, while other bulbs must be used only at such slow speeds as 1/25 or 1/30 second. For best results, each type of bulb should be used in a reflector of the right size and design. The jelly-bean-sized AG-1 bulb, for example, is most effective in a tiny 2-inch reflector. Walnut-sized No. 5 and 25 bulbs need a 4- or 5-inch reflector to take advantage of all the light they can put out.

To add to the confusion, different manufacturers use different numbers to designate similar bulbs. No. 5 and No. 25 bulbs are essentially the same bulb for our purposes, but they're made by different manufacturers.

But don't give up now! Fortunately, we can offer some fairly simple advice to bring order out of this apparent chaos. Almost all bulbs come in two colors, clear and blue. (The blue variety is designated by the letter "B" tacked onto its name—M5B, AG-1B, etc.) Blue or clear bulbs serve for black-and-white films. Blue bulbs must be used for daylight-type color films. This includes Kodacolor-X Film, unless the carton is marked "for clear flash."

Here is a simple formula for making good flash pictures without learning bulb designations and facts behind flash synchronization. If you have a box or non-adjustable camera, assume that if the bulb fits your flash holder, it will work with your camera. Then use the exposure information printed on the flash holder, in the instruction manual, or on the flash-bulb carton itself.

If you have an adjustable camera, start out by checking your instruction manual to see which bulbs can be used at which shutter speeds. Then buy the right kind of bulbs and forget all the rest. Figure your exposure settings from charts or from the table of flash guide numbers listed in this chapter. As long as you use the right bulb and figure your exposures as we've suggested, you can't go wrong!

You don't really have to know the *why* of flash, just the *how*. But if you're one of those insatiably curious types who must know the intricacies of flash synchronization, we commend the Kodak Data Book *Flash Pictures,* sold by Kodak dealers.

FLASH-BULB TYPES AND SYNCHRONIZATION

Flash-Bulb Base	Bulbs for Simple Cameras	Flash Bulbs for Most Cameras with Adjustable Shutters		
		At 1/25 or 1/30 sec	At Higher Shutter Speeds M sync	X sync
Screw	11, 40	11, 40, 2, 22	11, 40, 2, 22	None
Bayonet	SM, SF	5, 25	5, 25	SM, SF
Miniature	M2, M25	M2, M3, M5	M5	M2, M3
Baseless	AG-1	AG-1		

Note: If a flash-holder socket accepts both miniature and bayonet-base bulbs, the miniature bulb is preferable.

EXPOSURE SETTINGS FOR FLASH PICTURES

Lens apertures at various distances. Shutter at 1/25 or 1/30.

	Shallow Cylindrical Reflector	Inter-mediate Shape Reflector	Polished Bowl Shaped Reflector	Inter-mediate Shape Reflector	Polished Bowl Shaped Reflector
Flash to Subject Distance in Feet	**FLASH BULBS**			**FLASH BULBS**	
	AG1B		M2B	M3B M5B 5B 25B	

KODACOLOR-X, KODACHROME-X and
EKTACHROME-X—Daylight Type Films

$4\frac{1}{2}$	$f11$	$f16$	$f22$	$f22$	—
$6\frac{1}{2}$	8	11	16	16	22
9	5.6	8	11	11	16
13	4	5.6	8	8	11
18	2.8	4	5.6	5.6	8
26	2	2.8	4	4	5.6
35	—	2	2.8	2.8	4

KODACHROME II FILM

$3\frac{1}{2}$	$f8$	$f11$	$f16$	$f16$	$f22$
5	5.6	8	11	11	16
7	4	5.6	8	8	11
10	2.8	4	5.6	5.6	8
14	2	2.8	4	4	5.6
20	—	2	2.8	2.8	4
28	—	—	2	2	2.8

Flash exposures and guide numbers

The nearer anything is to a source of illumination, no matter whether that source be the sun or a tiny photoflash lamp, the greater the amount of illumination that will reach it. A person three feet away from a flash lamp is bathed in four times as much light as someone six feet away, and sixteen times as much as someone a dozen feet distant.

Since the amount of light available for picture taking does vary so extensively at different distances from its source, it seems only logical that camera exposures for flash shots (and for photoflood-lighted ones, too) depend on the actual distance from flash to subject.

The effectiveness of the flash reflector is also important. The deep bowl-shaped, highly polished reflectors usually concentrate practically all of the light from the flash bulb onto your subject. On the other hand, the very compact and shallow reflectors used with many modern cameras and flasholders allow more of the light to spill out to the sides and around the subject. This gives a softer lighting, but means that you need to use a longer lens opening than you would with a deeper bowl-shaped reflector.

The instruction sheet for each film has a table showing "guide numbers" for the various flash lamps with which it is usually employed. If you divide the guide number by the approximate number of feet from flash-to-subject, the number resulting will be the lens opening to use.

The table on the opposite page can save you some of this mental arithmetic, since it shows the lens openings to use at various distances, for several combinations of films, flash bulbs, and reflector shapes.

Shutter times for flash shots should be chosen, as they are outdoors, primarily in terms of action-stopping. When planning on a very brief one, however, it pays to check

137

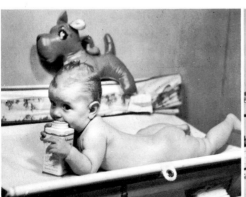

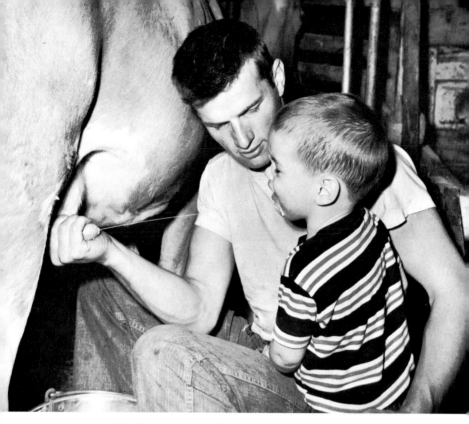

The flash lamp, itself, can often freeze expressions that would be altogether too fleeting for the camera's briefest shutter time. An SM or SF lamp in a box camera captured this one.

your camera manual for confirmation that your shutter will synchronize at that setting. With a rangefinder-type camera, you'll be able to work fastest with guide numbers if you first set the shutter time, then focus, and then divide the focusing distance into the guide number to obtain the lens opening.

Box-camera owners will notice that the flash data for their equipment, such as that given on the top of Kodak flash-holder reflectors, lists a range of distances in which a picture can be snapped with a stated flash lamp and film. Negative films have sufficient latitude that good prints can be made if the subject is anywhere within the range.

Avoiding flash failures

Disheartening as it may be, a snapshooter can choose the appropriate flash lamp, make the correct camera settings, even observe the lamp firing, and still find himself possessing a segment of film barren of exposure.

The batteries used in flash holders, much like us poor mortals, age whether they work or not. Even past their prime, a pair of these batteries may still be capable of flashing a lamp, but it takes them a greater length of time to do it. The extent of their tardiness may be only 1/50 second, but often this is enough to make your picture effort a complete whiff. Worse yet, anyone could conceivably shoot several rolls of important flash pictures before ever seeing a processed roll and discovering the awful truth.

There are two possible solutions. One is to replace your flash-holder batteries every three months. The other is to replace the batteries entirely with a battery-condenser unit, such as the Kodak B-C Flashpak. This gadget often preserves its battery component for more than two years and will provide either a good, positive, on-time flash or none at all.

Flash on and off the camera

Shooting with your flash holder mounted either on, alongside, or above your camera is, beyond all doubt, the easiest, quickest, and most popular means of obtaining an acceptable indoor photograph. Chances are that if such a convenient method of making indoor snapshots had never been devised, most people just plain wouldn't make them.

The number of things than can conceivably go wrong in flash-on-the-camera snapping form not only an extremely brief list but a rather untroublesome one. Backgrounds should always be checked before pressing the button just to be certain you aren't aiming directly at glass or some other highly reflective surface that's likely to cause a flared reflection of the flash. It's also a good idea to keep subjects at least a couple of feet away from a background wall so that their shadows won't form a distracting frame behind them. Another important point is to snap from at least the same level as the subject's head. Any light aimed upward will produce an unflattering effect and, if carried to an extreme, can turn even the pleasantest visage into something that looks like a creation of Dr. Frankenstein.

The only other vital point is that a fairly accurate estimate of camera-to-subject distance must be made to assure correct exposure. With a rangefinder-type camera, this presents no problem. Without a rangefinder, there are still some highly effective ways of "guess-timating" by employing units of measure that are easy to visualize. For longer distances, picture your own height laid out on the ground once, twice, or three times; for shorter ones, think in terms of arms' lengths which, for most people, are around 2½ feet.

The only real shortcoming of flash-on-the-camera snapping is that, like many convenient ways of doing things, it doesn't handle the job quite as well as it can be done. Pictures of people tend to have a somewhat pasty, flat look, because everything the camera lens sees of a subject gets an equal dose of light. This eliminates nearly all shadows, and shadows create the illusion of shape and dimension.

Merely extending the flash holder out high and to one side of the camera can increase snapshot quality appreciably. In the picture of the quartet, the lamp was fired from the right; in the one of the baby, from the left.

140

With a long enough flash extension cord—Kodak supplies a 20-foot length—you might even attempt unusual effects like this. Here, the flash holder was placed in the refrigerator so that it appears as if the picture was made by the refrigerator's light. Flash holders can also be placed this way in fireplaces to simulate shots made by firelight.

Even shifting the position of the flash holder by removing it from the camera and holding it at arm's length high and off to a 45-degree angle helps in this regard since it throws slightly less light on one side of a subject's face than on the other. This flash-off-the-camera technique can't be applied with box cameras, but with many adjustable-type cameras, the only required piece of additional equipment is an inexpensive flash extension cord. Exposure settings for a lamp fired in this way will be the same as they are for flash-on-the-camera, except in close-up shooting when the change in flash-to-subject distance may, percentage-wise, be sizeable. You'll find, too, that flash-off-the-camera demands a fair degree of manual dexterity since your camera must be operated entirely in one hand, but some cameras, particularly twin-lens reflex types, aren't especially difficult to maneuver in this way.

Needless to say, for every improvement in quality you achieve, you must pay with some loss in ease and convenience. It's merely a matter of deciding which brand of compromise suits you best.

Flash illumination bounced off a ceiling produces pictures in which shadows are thin and the background is as evenly lighted as the foreground, something difficult to achieve with one lamp.

Flash hits the ceiling

A picture taker who aims his flash lamp anywhere but directly at his subject might seem headed for a miss as wide as the circus fat lady. It's often possible, though, to achieve remarkably good results by firing that lamp at the ceiling instead of the subject.

This technique, called "bounce flash," demands that the ceiling in use be smooth, white or near white, and not much higher than the eight feet standard in most houses and apartments. The flash holder can be aimed from any point between floor and ceiling, but about halfway is generally best. As the light reflects from the ceiling, it spreads evenly throughout the room and fills it in almost the way that sunlight fills the outdoors. The one big and happy dif-ference, however, is that bounced light keeps bouncing off all four walls so that it eliminates the heavy directional shadows of bright sunlight.

Bounce flash will work only with adjustable cameras, because the flash holder must be removed from the camera. The most convenient means of exploiting this lighting system is to clamp your flash holder to the back of a chair with the ubiquitous Kodak Flexiclamp and attach it to your camera using a long flash extension cord so that you can wander freely at the end of this tether.

You'll be able to obtain good black-and-white shots almost anywhere in a room, except where the subject is directly between you and the flash. For color pictures, you must snap with the flash directly behind you and also be certain that neither the flash nor the subject is near a colored wall.

Exposure for bounce-flash shooting doesn't depend nearly so much on flash-to-subject distance as it does on the size and characteristics of the room in which you are working. For one of medium size (about 10 by 12 feet) with a white ceiling, the following settings for an M5 lamp will be a good jumping-off point:

FILM with clear or blue bulbs	Trial Settings	FILM with blue bulbs	Trial Settings
Verichrome Pan	1/50, ƒ22	Kodachrome II, Daylight	1/50, ƒ5.6
Panatomic-X	1/50, ƒ11	Kodachrome-X	1/25, ƒ11
		Ektachrome-X	1/25, ƒ11
Tri-X Pan	1/50, ƒ22	Kodacolor-X	1/25, ƒ11

While these will probably deliver satisfactory exposures in most locations, the only means of being absolutely certain of your settings in any room is to try a brief experimental series of shots. In the first, use a lens setting two openings larger than the one suggested above; in the next, one larger; then, the suggested trial setting; and, finally, both a full opening smaller and two full openings smaller. Whichever produces the best snapshot should be given a chance to prove itself over a greater variety of pictures in that particular room. Once it has, you can continue to apply it in that room unless the wall or ceiling colors are changed drastically.

You'll probably find that exposure requirements in a large room will demand a lens setting a half-opening larger than in a room of medium size, and also that pictures made down close to the floor require a half-opening larger than those exposed at standing or sitting levels.

Ordinarily, it would be necessary to use three flash lamps for lighting as even and devoid of heavy shadows as this. The picture, though, was made by bouncing one off the ceiling.

143

More than one lamp

If a rabbit originated the thought that when one is good, two must be better, and three even better than that, he probably realized, too late, that the unlimited application of such reasoning can become entirely unmanageable. The same idea, but kept within definite limits, applies to flash photography. Two lights certainly can produce better results than one, and three lights can be better than two, but the use of multiple-flash setups depends upon the kind of subject being snapped and on whether the value of the picture justifies the additional cost and effort.

Only a subject that will pretty well remain in one location is suitable for multiple-flash shooting, since the lighting arrangement is relatively immobile. Extra equipment required for multiple flash consists of one or more extension flash holders and a battery-condenser power unit in the flash holder that's connected to the camera shutter. Metal lamp stands are a good addition to your photographic kit if you use multiple flash frequently and if you have difficulty recruiting sufficient human lamp stands. For once-in-a-while operations, the versatile Kodak Flexiclamp works well.

Although the second lamp in a two-lamp setup can be exploited for any purpose, the most common placement has one light high, off to one side of the camera, and aiming down at the subject, with the other one 45 degrees away and on the other side of the camera. The second lamp should be at the same level as the subject. For color snap-

144

In a two-lamp setup, it's best to locate your lamps as shown here. With color films, both should be the same distance from the subject; with black-and-white, one should be a third farther away than the other.

Once there was a bulldog named "George" who liked to play poker but wasn't especially good at it. When he did win, though, he certainly lorded it objectionably, as you can see . . . In picture situations like this, when you can be fairly certain of keeping your subject or subjects in the same location, multiple flash can be employed to provide an extra measure of quality.

The expressions on a child's face shift with amazing rapidity, but the illumination produced by an electronic flash unit has such a short duration that it can capture even the most fleeting look.

shots, results are usually better when the two lamps are the same distance from the subject; in black-and-white shooting, you will get a more rounded, three-dimensional photograph if the second lamp is about one-third farther back than the first. To calculate exposure for an arrangement like this, merely figure it for the first lamp alone, and then close the lens by half an opening.

Electronic flash equipment

An electronic flash unit is simply a collection of electrical components that enable a special "lamp" to produce 10,000 or more flashes rather than the mere one of a conventional flash lamp. A good one isn't an inexpensive piece of equipment, but it can be an economical investment. Portable electronic flash outfits will cost about as much as a good adjustable camera but if you do a fair amount of flash snapping, in the range of 150 to 200 or more shots a year, it will soon pay for itself in flash-lamp savings.

The burst of light from a portable electronic unit is much briefer than that from a flash lamp. It usually has a

And if anything is harder to catch than a child's expression, it's a cat's. The 1/500 to 1/2000-second flash of an electronic outfit makes this a cinch, though, if you snap at the right moment.

duration of from 1/500 to 1/2000 second, depending upon the type and power supply. This insures extremely sharp pictures, even of fast-moving subjects, and helps capture photogenic but fleeting facial expressions.

These devices cannot be fired machine-gun style, since time must be allowed for the batteries or rectifier to recharge the power-storing condenser. This, however, seldom takes more than a few seconds.

Illumination produced by electronic flash units approximates the color of daylight and so is ideally suited for making indoor pictures on Daylight Type color films.

Synchronization is entirely different than for any type of flash lamp. The action of most electronic equipment is so immediate and its burst of light so quick that the camera shutter must actually be opened before the electronic unit is triggered. This is called "X-synchronization" and, without it, a camera cannot operate satisfactorily with electronic flash. Most recent adjustable cameras, however, do have shutters that are X-synchronized. A few of these flash outfits have a delay built into them which adapts them

Electronic-flash illumination approximates the color of daylight. Most units don't necessitate a filter with daylight-type color films.

to the same M-synchronization as is used with No. 5 and No. 25 flash lamps. The instruction booklet packed with an electronic unit will mention the correct "synch" to employ.

For more about electronic equipment, see a copy of the Kodak Data Book, *Flash Pictures.*

A simplified approach

Sunlight is just as free indoors as out. While it may not be quite as plentiful, there's enough of it in most rooms on a bright day for easy black-and-white picture taking with any adjustable camera.

Although the financial attractions of this sort of photography may seem predominant, there are other advantages equally outstanding. Whenever a flash lamp is fired, it unmistakably announces the presence of a camera and this often makes prospective subjects wary or uncomfortable. In flashless snap shooting, however, a camera is relatively unobtrusive. You'll also discover that pictures shot by existing light have an unusually pleasant appearance and a distinctive naturalness.

Actually, as light pours through windows and into a room, it tends to spread across that room rather unevenly. Even excluding those locations in direct sunlight (here you can shoot just as if you were outdoors), there are some areas that will receive four or eight times as much illumination as others.

If you prefer color pictures, Kodak High Speed Ektachrome Film is a natural because of its great speed. For black-and-white pictures, Kodak Tri-X Pan Film is so fast that you can shoot indoor pictures without flash on a bright day at settings well within the scope of all but box cameras. And Tri-X Pan has enormous exposure latitude, too.

Even color snapshots can often be made by the existing light. Kodak High Speed Ektachrome Film is preferable for this kind of shooting because of its great light-sensitivity.

149

In one part of a room there might be sufficient illumination so that, critically speaking, the best exposure would be 1/50, *f* 11. In another part, there might be so little that you'd need settings of 1/50, *f* 2.8. But with Tri-X Film in a camera set at 1/50, *f* 5.6, you'd probably get a printable negative if you snapped away with either setting.

The best way to gain an appreciation of what a wonderfully easy method this is for making fine, inexpensive snapshots is simply by trying it some sunny day. Set your camera at 1/50, *f* 5.6, or some equivalent exposure, and shoot any kind of pictures you wish. Try it in each room of your house. It's a good idea to turn the room lights on, not because they add a great deal of illumination but merely because they smooth out some of the sunlight's unevenness. If your camera, like the Kodak Duaflex with Kodar Lens, has its widest lens opening at *f* 8, chances are that results with Tri-X Film will be quite satisfactory, especially in light-walled rooms.

You'll probably find that all or nearly all of your prints will turn out wonderfully. If the pictures taken in one room should all be disappointing, take a look at the nega-

EXPOSURE LATITUDE

Negatives made on Kodak Tri-X Film at widely varying settings still yield good prints. This latitude is the chief reason that 1/50, *f* 5.6 will probably give you good indoor pictures in almost any room on a sunny day. These were all exposed in a brightly lighted bathroom with a shutter time of 1/25 second.

NEGATIVES

f 2   *f* 2.8   *f* 4

PRINTS

tives. When they appear extremely transparent, try settings of 1/50, f 3.5 or f 2.8 in that room. When they are black and heavy, shift to 1/50, f 11. Once you have hit upon settings that yield good pictures in a certain room on a sunny day, you can count on their always doing equally well under the same conditions.

Approximate Tri-X settings for some other common picture locations and subjects are:

Brightly lit interiors of public buildings . . . . 1/50, f 4.5
Spot-lit athletic, stage or ice show . . . . 1/200, f 2
Home interiors, bright artificial light . . . . . . 1/25, f 3.5
Television pictures . . . . 1/25, f 4.5
Brightly lit downtown areas at night . . . . . . 1/25, f 3.5

Because exposure for color films is more critical, you'd better use an exposure meter with High Speed Ektachrome.

Flashless shooting in any location

A living room or a kitchen on a bright day is a fairly standardized situation, not quite so much as the pure outdoor ones listed on film instruction sheets and on the Kodaguide Snapshot Dial, but near enough so that Tri-X Pan Film's marvelous exposure latitude can bridge whatever variations occur.

On other kinds of days, at other times of day, in other locations, and with other kinds of film, it's much more difficult to guess exposure settings. With color films, it's nearly impossible due to their relatively slim latitude.

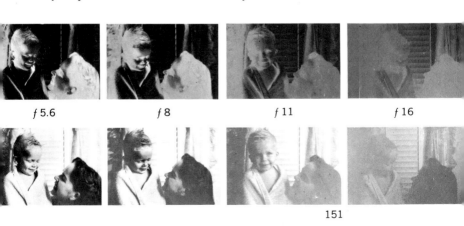

f 5.6 f 8 f 11 f 16

SHOOT COLOR ANYWHERE—
WITHOUT FLASH
Almost anywhere you go with your camera it's possible to bring back a memorable collection of color pictures without resorting to flash. These shots were made during a tour of the famous Glass Center of the Corning Glass Works.

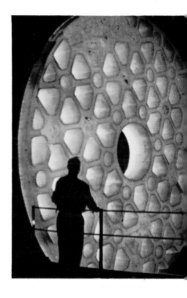

Pictures like these demonstrate the soft, pleasant quality of existing light. Although they represent a wide variety of locations, all were shot on sunny days and, with Kodak Tri-X Film, could have been captured at exposure settings of 1/50, f 5.6.

But fine indoor snapshots *can* be made without flash in almost any location, even in color. Color pictures exposed by existing light have, in fact, a particularly attractive quality.

The only problem is one of acquiring workable exposure data, and this necessitates actually measuring the amount of light available in each prospective picture location. This is the job done by an exposure meter. It's as an aid in indoor shooting of this kind that a meter is really most useful. How exposure meters operate and are employed is covered in the section beginning on page 162.

When a young lady goes shopping, your camera, if loaded with Tri-X Film, can follow right along. These were shot in a market at 1/50, *f* 5.6.

Camera steadiness in long hand-held exposures

Pictures snapped by fairly dim existing light rarely look quite as sharp as those made under a bright, unclouded sky. The inevitable need for wide lens openings which reduce the range of sharp focus and exaggerate focusing errors is partially responsible, but only partially. Careless and casual use of comparatively long shutter times also takes its toll.

Nearly all outdoor shooting is done with the shutter set at 1/50 second, 1/100 second, or even a briefer interval of time. At such settings, slight camera shake may not become readily apparent unless a negative is greatly enlarged or a slide projected to extreme dimensions. At 1/25 second or longer, though, any slight tremor makes itself much more evident.

It isn't always essential that a shutter time of 1/25 second or longer be used for snapping by existing light. Whenever it can be avoided, it should be. But often, when the illumination level is low, such a shutter time may mean the difference between picture and no picture. Placing your camera on a tripod or Kodak Flexiclamp would, of course, eliminate any problem of unsteadiness, but a tripod also eliminates one of the great merits of shooting by existing light—its spontaneity.

A few means of promoting maximum possible camera steadiness for hand-held exposures are:

Hold your arms close in against your sides.

Brace an eye-level type camera firmly against your cheek.

Hold a waist-level-type camera slightly away from your body, but so that the neckstrap is taut.

Take a deep breath, exhale, hold your breath, then shoot.

Squeeze the button gently.

If you can discover a convenient wall, table, or other solid object against which to hold your camera or even merely to lean, it will be of considerable help in maintaining reasonable picture sharpness for exposures of 1/25, 1/10, or even 1/5 second.

On some occasions, particularly when the needle on a light meter won't even twitch, it may be worth a gamble to open the lens as wide as it will go, try the longest shutter time you dare, and then just trust to luck.

A silhouette simply requires the correct exposure for the background. It's especially easy when you can use an outdoor scene for background.

After dark, indoor illumination varies so much that it's almost impossible to guess exposure. In situations like this, an exposure meter is essential.

The fundamentals of floods

Since photoflood lamps must be plugged into some source of electrical current, they never quite match the versatility of flash bulbs. Anyone trying hopefully to illuminate an active two- or four-legged subject with a flood may soon find himself in the same predicament as a dog on a 25-foot rope pouncing on a bone 26 feet away.

But in their own field of operation, the lighting of subjects that can be depended upon to stay put, flood lamps offer some mighty attractive advantages, not the least of them being economy. A flash lamp's useful life is measured in fractions of a second, but even the shortest-lived photoflood will shine forth for three hours, and most floods will last even longer.

Auxiliary equipment is also simple and inexpensive. Using photoflood lamps which have built-in reflectors, it can be as makeshift as a few old lamp bases. For something slightly less makeshift, you can either buy or rig up some special gadgets which combine a long extension cord, a lamp socket, and a pressure clamp for positioning each flood.

Another point in favor of photofloods is that they permit the picture taker to see exactly what effect his lights are creating, something only an experienced practitioner can visualize with flash illumination. Once a person has become accustomed to the idea that the very lightest shadows will appear much darker in his final picture, he can shift his floods around with considerable success.

The color of the light produced by photofloods is much yellower than daylight. This does not cause any difficulty with Kodacolor Film but it requires the use of blue correction filters for pictures on Daylight Type color slide films. Unfortunately this cuts down the effective speed of the film, so that it is generally more practical to use a film, such as Kodachrome II Professional, Type A, which is balanced for photoflood light.

Photofloods consume an enormous amount of electricity. More than three on the same circuit will often blow the fuse.

156

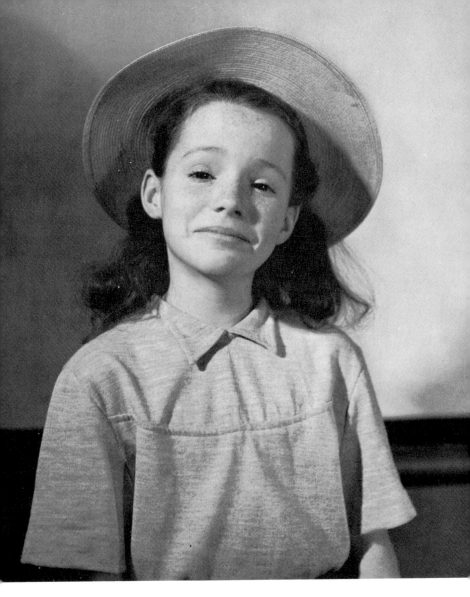

Whether the expression is smiling or smug, as long as the person
behind it will remain in one location for a few moments, photoflood lamps provide a flexible, inexpensive means of illumination.

Arrangement and exposure

A lone photoflood lamp will create about the same sort of picture quality as a single flash lamp. While there's nothing objectionable about this, it isn't much more strenuous for anyone who's maneuvering one lamp to engineer a two-lamp setup and take advantage of the tremendous quality dividend it makes possible.

In the most versatile two-lamp floodlighting arrangement for photographing people, one lamp is located to the

A single lamp alongside the camera gives the flat lighting typical of flash-on-the-camera shooting.

When the lamp is moved farther to the side and aimed down, the shadows created are too dark.

left of the camera and the other to the right, with a gap of about 45 degrees separating them. One of these lamps, and it doesn't make much difference which one, should be aimed down on the subject, with the other kept at head height.

In color snapping, the distance from lamp to subject should be identical for both lamps; with black-and-white films, the lamp at head height should be one-third farther back than the other lamp.

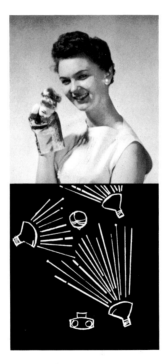

Another lamp 45 degrees to the right but farther away will make the shadows lighter and pleasant.

A third lamp, when aimed solely at the background, will often contribute to better picture quality.

Especially for pictures of women, a third lamp may be aimed down at the hair to produce highlights.

Pictures can be snapped at any distance from the subject, since camera settings are determined by the position of the lamps rather than of the camera. Some basic settings for this two-lamp system are:

KODAK COLOR FILMS

Lamp-to-Subject Distance (in feet)	Kodachrome II Prof, Type A	Kodacolor
4½ feet	1/50 or 1/60, ƒ 4	1/25, ƒ 4.5
6 feet	1/50 or 1/60, ƒ 2.8	1/25, ƒ 3.5
9 feet	1/50 or 1/60, ƒ 2	

KODAK BLACK-AND-WHITE FILMS

Lamp-to-Subject Distances (in feet)	Panatomic-X	Verichrome Pan Plus-X	Tri-X
5 and 7	1/25, ƒ 4	1/50, ƒ 5.6	1/50, ƒ 8
7 and 10	1/25, ƒ 2.8	1/50, ƒ 4	1/50, ƒ 5.6

A complete photoflood computer, providing camera settings at all lamp-to-subject distances, is included in the Kodak Master photoguide.

There's no authoritarian book of rules on snap shooting that decrees a certain photoflood lamp must be located in such-and-such position and none other. Picture taking is a highly permissive pastime, and no source of illumination could be more suitable as an outlet for someone's creative and/or tinkering instincts than floods.

Illustrations and charts can only suggest a handful of the potentialities offered by various positionings and combinations. Your own curiosity and your eyes can tell you much more.

The only piece of extra equipment needed for this kind of experimentation is an exposure meter. Without a meter, the correct exposure settings for any special arrangement of lights would be as difficult to assess as they are under dim existing light.

When shooting by photofloods, always seek your exposure setting by the incident light method since a reflected light reading is likely to be disproportionately influenced by dark, underilluminated backgrounds or surrounding areas and give you data that is quite likely to cause severe overexposure.

160

For floodlighted shots of children and/or pets, Kodak Tri-X Film
is especially advantageous. It permits you to employ a shutter
time as brief as 1/100 second while still maintaining a lens opening small enough to provide a comfortable range of sharpness.

161

When they are needed

As long as the sun shines forth, outdoor picture taking becomes, literally, a snap. All essential exposure data is available in easy-to-use, reliable aids like the film instruction sheets and the Kodaguide Snapshot Dial. But desirable snapshot situations often occur in deep shade, late in the day, or under dark, cloudy skies, conditions which make exposure guessing a chancy occupation.

Indoors, the same sort of difficulty looms when you try to make pictures, particularly in color, by natural, existing light or by photofloods.

What's needed is a device that will actually measure the amount of illumination and convert the measurement into terms of camera settings. This is precisely the function of an exposure meter.

How they work

Ordinary light can be converted into electricity, not in sufficient amounts to brew a pot of coffee or even stimulate a toy train, but enough to push an indicator needle over a small arc. The tiny device performing this virtuoso feat of applied physics is a photoelectric cell and the brighter the light shining upon it, the greater the current created and the farther the needle will jump.

A cell like this, with a numerical scale behind the needle, is at the heart of all exposure meters. In some meters the digits on the scale are actual lens openings; in others, they have little significance in themselves.

To obtain valid exposure data from any meter, you must provide it with the shutter time you plan to use and with a key number called the film exposure index.

Film Speeds

On the instruction sheets accompanying rolls of Kodak film is a mysterious inscription that may look something like this: "Speed ASA 400." It's not really mysterious at all. Speed refers to the speed of the film—how fast it is, that is, how sensitive to light. ASA stands for American Standards Association, the group that lays the ground rules for measuring such things. The number "400" is the speed of the film . . . in this case, Kodak Tri-X Pan Film. That's the number you set on your light meter or automatic camera to get the right lens and shutter settings.

Some kinds of film are more sensitive to light than others, and the speed numbers are simply numerical expressions of this sensitivity. For example, Kodak Tri-X Pan Film, with its speed of 400, is ten times more light-sensitive than Kodak Panatomic-X Film, which has a speed of 40. In other words, it takes ten times as much light to capture a scene on Panatomic-X as on Tri-X—a difference of over three lens openings.

How to use speed numbers

With meters that read directly in ƒ-numbers, your intended shutter time and the film's speed number should be set on the meter before making your light reading. With other meters, you make your reading first and then feed it and the film speed into a computer which gives you a choice of several shutter time and lens opening combinations, all of which will give proper exposure.

Generally speaking, you'll obtain a high percentage of good pictures by adhering to the published speed numbers and the meter manufacturer's instructions. Sometimes, though, your particular meter or camera or the kind of subject you photograph most often may need some shift from the published speeds. If, for example, all of your color slides are slightly but consistently underexposed (on the dark side), the easiest way to correct this is by using a smaller film speed. With Ektachrome-X Film, instead of employing the published speed of 64, you might try the next smaller value that appears on your meter, 50 or even 40. Once you discover a speed that repeatedly provides satisfactory results, stay with it.

With black-and-white films, use larger proportional changes. Should your negatives be constantly too dense (overexposed), double or even quadruple the speed you are employing.

For more information on meters and film speeds, see the Data Book *Kodak Films*.

Reflected light readings are best when it's inconvenient or impossible to get into the same location or light as the picture subject. They are made by pointing the meter cell toward the subject.

Incident light readings must be made in the same light that is falling on the subject. The meter cell should be pointed half-way between the light source and the snapping position.

Two ways of light measurement

Light can be measured either as it travels toward a picture subject (incident light method) or as it is reflected from a subject (reflected light method). Most meters are designed primarily for one or the other of these methods but many of the new ones adapt to both.

Incident light readings must be made from the same location as the subject or, at least, in the same light. If the chief source of illumination is on the same side of the subject as the position from which you'll be snapping, point the meter about half-way between the light source and your intended camera position; if the source is behind the subject, the meter should be aimed directly toward the spot where you'll be shooting.

Reflected light measurements can usually be made from your snapping position by merely pointing the meter toward the subject.

Using a meter outdoors

The simplest and usually the best way to use a meter outdoors is the reflected light method. On a dull kind of day when meters are most helpful, always aim the meter cell low. Gradually move it up. When it begins to "see" the comparatively bright sky, the needle will rise rapidly. Base your exposure settings only on the reading obtained before the needle jumped. You'll find other helpful tips on outdoor meter use in your meter instruction manual.

Using meters indoors

For shooting indoor pictures by existing light, first try a reading by the more convenient reflected light method. If the illumination is so dim that the meter needle moves only slightly or not at all, shift to an incident light reading since many meters are more sensitive used in this way. When you change from one system to the other, be sure to follow directions. If you treat an incident light reading as though it was a reflected light reading, you will seriously underexpose your picture.

When shooting by photofloods, always seek your exposure setting by the incident light method since a reflected light reading is likely to be disproportionately influenced by dark, underilluminated backgrounds or surrounding areas and give you data that will cause overexposure.

165

How color gets into a color picture

Black-and-white film, pared down to its most essential elements, is simply a platform of clear, flexible plastic support about 3/1000-inch thick, with a much slimmer layer of light-sensitive photographic emulsion resting on it. After exposure and processing, a negative silver image of the picture becomes fixed in this slender coating of emulsion.

Reversal color films, such as Kodachrome and Ektachrome, in which the final color photograph appears on the film used in the camera, really contain three separate pictures on one support. On the same platform are a trio of piggy-backed emulsion layers, each of them contributing one primary color. These are black-and-white emulsions, not basically unlike those in Verichrome Pan, Tri-X, and other black-and-white films.

Just as nearly all colors of paint can be mixed from three pigments, all colors in a color photograph are produced by combinations of three dyes—yellow, cyan (a light blue-green), and magenta (a pinkish blue-red). These correspond roughly to the yellow, so-called blue (actually a blue-green), and so-called red (really a blue-red) paints in a child's watercolor set. The dyes used in color photographs, however, are much purer than any paints and are capable of reproducing a wider range of tones.

The topmost layer of a Kodachrome or Ektachrome slide has a positive yellow image of everything in the picture that is yellow or that needs yellow in its color mixture. The middle layer contains a magenta image, and the bottom layer, a cyan image. These three pictures, when viewed together, form the complete color transparency, with all of its varied, delicate, and subtle hues.

How the right amount of the right dye gets into the right place in the right layer is, of course, the great techni-

166

cal marvel of color films. A complete explanation would go far beyond the scope of this book, but, in very brief terms, this is what happens:

The top emulsion layers of Kodachrome and Ektachrome films are sensitive to only that part of white light that is controlled by their yellow dye. If you should snap a picture and develop these color films in much the same way as ordinary black-and-white films, you would have in this layer a typical negative image composed of minute particles of silver. Since this would be a negative image, the remaining area of this emulsion layer must represent a positive of the yellow parts of the picture. A dye of very pure yellow color is then formed in all of the emulsion layer not occupied by the negative silver image and, after it is solidly established, the silver is removed. In a similar manner, the positive magenta image is formed in the middle layer, and the cyan image, in the bottom layer.

For a more detailed discussion of color and color films and particularly on how color images are formed, consult *Color As Seen and Photographed,* a Kodak Data Book sold by most Kodak dealers.

Color couplers and what they do

When anyone purchases a roll of Kodachrome or Kodak Ektachrome Film, he buys hardly a whit of color. The actual dyes which eventually form the picture never come into existence until the film is processed, and even then, only about mid-way in the processing cycle.

The substances most instrumental in producing these dyes are called "couplers," and there is a different coupler for yellow, cyan, and magenta. Only when each of them finally couples to a chemical produced by the color developer do they blossom forth into their characteristic hues.

One of the major differences between Kodachrome and Ektachrome Films is that the couplers employed in Ektachrome are placed in the appropriate emulsion layers during manufacture of the film. Those in Kodachrome enter the film during processing, requiring a separate and critical step for each. This is chiefly responsible for the fact that Kodachrome processing demands complex and carefully controlled equipment, while Ektachrome Film can be successfully processed in any kitchen sink with a few simple working tools.

Daylight Type and Types A & B—
why we have both

The human eye, normally as discriminating an appraiser as anyone might wish, does its best to ignore a phenomenon it encounters almost continuously and one that's a highly critical factor in color snap shooting. Our eyes simply gloss over the fact that there's a considerable difference between the color of daylight and the color of incandescent light.

The illumination produced by an ordinary household light bulb has a definite yellow cast when compared with daylight. Photoflood illumination is slightly less yellowish, and clear flash lamps throw out a light just a bit less yellow than floods, but all of these lighting sources group into the same general family.

Daylight, however, has a comparatively blue color which is pretty nearly duplicated by blue-coated flash lamps and electronic flash equipment.

While the eye can and largely does accommodate this difference, color film cannot. A film manufactured to provide the most pleasing color results possible under daylight will inevitably show a strong over-all yellowness if exposed by clear flash lamps. On the other hand, when a film attuned to clear flash illumination is exposed by daylight, the transparencies will be heavily blue.

In the case of color negative films, such as Kodacolor Film, the difference caused by the color quality of the light source can be balanced out in the printing step. With color slide films, however, it is necessary to use light balancing filters or else to use films that are balanced for the different light sources. Kodachrome II Professional Film, Type A, is balanced for use with photoflood lamps. Type B films, such as Kodak High Speed Ektachrome Film, Type B, are balanced for the somewhat yellower 3200 K studio lamps, but will also give quite pleasing results with the still yellower light from household lamps.

THE INSIDE STORY

Color films have three piggy-back layers of light-sensitive emulsion. The top one reacts to blue light; the middle one, to green; and the bottom, to red. What happens in each of these layers during processing is shown in this exaggerated cross section.

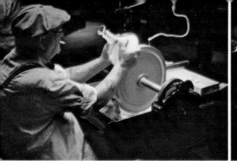

In mixed illumination, part daylight and part tungsten, daylight-type films (left) give a warm over-all balance; type A films, a cool balance. Both would probably be acceptable to most people.

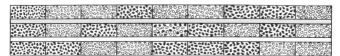

Let's say your picture subject has a wide range of colors which, for simplicity's sake, we can represent with these color patches.

After black-and-white development, all areas in the top layer exposed to blue or partly blue colors become negative silver images. The same thing occurs in the middle layer wherever there was any green in the subject, and in the bottom layer where there was red.

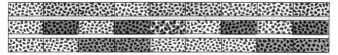

During color development, all previously unexposed and undeveloped areas are simultaneously developed (they form a positive image) and occupied by appropriate dyes. These dyes are yellow in the top layer, magenta in the middle, cyan the bottom.

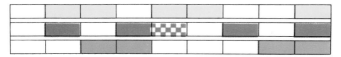

Then all silver images are removed, leaving behind a positive color representation made up of superimposed dye images.

169

The why and how of a Kodacolor negative

Reversal-type color films, such as Kodachrome and Kodak Ektachrome, are rather demanding photographic servants. They show little tolerance for human error, and whenever a pair of exposure settings fails to satisfy their requirements by the extent of as little as one lens opening, the effect on picture quality is severe and readily apparent. Much of this is due to the most basic characteristic of reversal materials, that the film in the camera and the final picture are one and the same piece of film. Fortunately, Kodachrome and Ektachrome are primarily used in cameras capable of varying exposure settings to meet changes in illumination conditions and the most frequently encountered conditions are quite easy to recognize.

The negative-positive system, in color as in black-and-white, offers a great deal more flexibility. Negative-type color films, such as Kodacolor, and their color printing papers combine to provide greater exposure latitude than reversal color films. Although there is one certain bright-

sun exposure that will contribute to the most desirable picture quality for Kodachrome and Ektachrome Films, Kodacolor has an exposure range equivalent to three *f*-openings. A negative exposed anywhere within that range will produce a good print.

This, naturally, is crucial to owners of box cameras, because they have no means of adjusting their lens opening and shutter time to meet varying conditions.

Although a negative may have received somewhat less exposure than is really desirable, it may still contain sufficient detail and suitable color for a good print. If it were printed in exactly the same manner as a better, more fully exposed negative (the equivalent of what occurs in reversal-film processing), the print would probably be a poor one. However, if the printing exposure is adjusted to the needs of each individual negative, the final picture will not only be acceptable but may be virtually indistinguishable from one made by a better negative. This depends, of course, on the negative itself, and also on the skill of the person operating the printing machine, but it is a definite and important plus for negative color films and, again, one especially important to box-camera snap shooters.

The advantages of the negative-positive kind of photographic process are easy to appreciate when you see that two negatives as different in appearance as those on the facing page can both, through variations in printing technique, yield prints as good as the one at the left.

The colors in a Kodacolor negative (above) are opposite those in the scene. Greens will be magenta, reds will be cyan, but, due to the over-all orange tint of the negative, much of this relationship isn't readily apparent.

Kodacolor Prints (at left) are all oversized prints. This is the actual size of one made from a 2¼ by 3¼-inch negative. All Kodacolor Prints are 3½ inches in width; their depth depends on the dimensions of the negative. The structure of the printing paper's emulsion is quite similar to that of the Kodacolor film.

Why a Kodacolor negative looks as it does

Technically and basically, the films manufactured for both the negative and reversal color processes are quite similar in construction. The top emulsion layer of Kodacolor Film, like that of reversal color films, is blue-sensitive and has a yellow filter coating beneath it. Also, the succeeding emulsions are green-sensitive and red-sensitive, respectively.

The major difference, though, is that the yellow dye enters the *same* portions of the top emulsion exposed by the blue areas of the subject. It replaces the tiny silver particles formed in the first step of processing. This makes a Kodacolor negative doubly negative. First, like a black-and-white negative, it is dark where the subject was light. Second, its colors are directly opposite those of the subject—yellowest where the subject was bluest, cyanest where it was reddest.

Some of these relationships are a little difficult to appreciate fully since they become lost in the characteristic dull-orange tint that covers all Kodacolor negatives. This orange color, however, contributes to the high quality of Kodacolor prints.

Slides from Kodacolor Negatives

You can order color slides from Kodacolor negatives in the 135 (full frame), 828 and 127 square sizes. See your Kodak dealer for details.

PRESERVING COLOR PICTURES

The dyes used in Kodak color films, although the most stable ones compatible with photographic requirements, may, in time, change. Appreciable shifts, however, can be reduced by avoiding contact with excesses of moisture, heat, and light.

The worst possible location for storage of slides, prints, and negatives is one that tends to chronic dampness. Most basements fall into this category. Not only will the moisture in the air affect the colors, but it will also contribute to the growth of surface fungus.

In most homes, a dark shelf in a closet or cabinet is likely to prove the most satisfactory repository for valued color pictures. If the building is a multi-story structure, the ground floor will generally remain cooler than upper levels and therefore be preferable. To preserve framed prints, merely keep them out of direct sunlight and keep the front surface of the print out of direct contact with the glass.

Where relative humidities of 60 percent or more prevail for long periods of time, it may be worthwhile to consider building an airtight box for your color pictures. Desiccating devices suitable for absorbing moisture in such boxes are sold in most photographic stores.

To preserve color slides, they should be kept in projection position only as long as absolutely required. Never use a projection lamp of greater wattage than recommended by the projector manufacturer, since such lamps produce a greater amount of heat than the projector's heat-absorbing glass is capable of handling.

Most finger marks and dirt can be removed from film surfaces with Kodak Film Cleaner, also available in most camera shops.

ORDERING COLOR PRINTS AND ENLARGEMENTS

All of the qualities that contribute toward making any Kodachrome or Kodak Ektachrome slide a good one—things like sharpness, accurate exposure, and picture interest—will help it yield equally good color prints. The only additional and special qualification is that the transparency not be of extremely high contrast, with large, important, heavy shadow areas.

Kodak dealers can provide a quick run-down on the various print sizes available and the prices thereof. You'll usually find that Kodachrome prints and enlargements will prove more economical if only one is required from each slide. For more than one print from the same slide, you'll save money by having a Kodacolor negative first produced from your transparency and ordering inexpensive Kodacolor prints and enlargements.

Unless a print has already been made from a Kodacolor negative, it is a little difficult for anyone but a trained photographic specialist to visualize the kind of print it will yield. Sharpness can be discerned from the negative, though, and is, of course, vital.

A Kodacolor negative that has already yielded a good

print will be likely to contribute to an even better enlargement. When ordering Kodacolor prints or enlargements, you can choose either to employ the entire negative or have a partial, cropped area of the negative fill the print. Your dealer can list the standard cropping dimensions and instruct you how to mark your negative for cropping.

These are both fine, well exposed, sharp slides. The top one would make an excellent color print. If the bottom one were printed, though, the shadow areas on the face would probably become even darker and cause the print to be disappointing.

HOW TO USE FILM INSTRUCTIONS

The film instruction sheet packaged with each roll of Kodak Film (except Verichrome Pan) is a laboratory-tested recipe for getting the best possible pictures. These sheets always contain the very latest information on the film with which they're packed. Instruction sheets vary a little bit, of course, depending on whether the film is black-and-white or color, but let's look at the major sections of an instruction sheet to make sure you know how to use all the help it contains.

The opening paragraph tells what the film is and what it's to be used for. Next is a section headed "Speed," which lists the number you set on your exposure meter or automatic camera. (See page 162.)

If you don't use an exposure meter, you'll find the "Daylight Exposure Table" helpful for finding the right camera settings for different kinds of daylight conditions, such as sunny or overcast days.

Flash guide numbers are listed to help you make well-exposed flash pictures with an adjustable camera. See pages 136 and 137 to make sure you know how to use guide numbers.

Along about here you'll find a section on filters, in a black-and-white instruction sheet, that shows how much exposure increase is needed with various filters.

Finally, there is a section that gives complete processing instructions for black-and-white films or tells you how to get your film processed, in the case of color films. The numbers on the very bottom of the back of the instruction sheet show you when it was published, by the way. "10-65," for example, would mean that a particular sheet was printed during October, 1965. If two instruction sheets conflict, use the newer one.

The arrow is pointing to the film speed dial of an automatic camera. This is where you set the ASA Speed for your film listed in the instruction sheet. This dial is set at 32, which is the speed of Koda-color Film.

How film becomes a negative

Photography, for all of its diversity and occasional complexity, with its f-numbers and color couplers, is anchored to a single, starkly simple manifestation of physics: that certain substances react physically to light and undergo distinct changes.

This same sort of reaction occurs in dozens of everyday objects as far removed from picture taking as small boys commonly are from bathtubs. A sheet of paper left in the sunlight will slowly yellow. Draperies gradually fade. Even photosynthesis, the process by which plants absorb carbon from carbon dioxide in the air and give off by-product oxygen, is triggered by light.

The light-sensitive material employed in photographic film, however, does not react visibly. It requires chemical development to produce something that can be seen and will be permanent. Back when the most common snapshot films could be handled safely under dim red illumination, you could easily observe that they looked exactly the same after exposure as before. The great advantage of such materials, though, is that they acquire their latent (or invisible) image on extremely brief exposure to light.

Key ingredient of a film emulsion is a compound in crystalline form called "silver bromide." When the camera shutter opens, a pattern of bright and dark areas representing the picture scene is projected through the lens and onto the film. A subtle change takes place in those crystals struck by light so that, when the film is placed in a developer solution, these and only these crystals are separated into the bromide, which is carried off with the developer, and black grains of silver. After a development time that is sufficient to develop all of the exposed crystals but not so long that the developer will begin acting upon unexposed crystals, the developer is poured off, the film rinsed, and a chemical "fixer" added. This removes all of the unexposed silver bromide and leaves a negative representation of the picture scene in which the densest collection of microscopic silver grains form the brightest areas and no silver at all appears where the picture scene reflected no light.

Exposure data—Kodak black-and-white films

Film	ASA Film Speeds
Panatomic-X (roll)	40
Panatomic-X (135)	32
Verichrome Pan	125
Plus-X Pan (35mm)	125
Tri-X Pan	400

Basic Exposure Settings at 1/100 Second

	Bright or Hazy Sun on Light Sand or Snow	Bright or Hazy Sun	Cloudy Bright No Shadows	Heavy Overcast	Open Shade
Verichrome Pan Film	f22	f16	f8	f5.6	f5.6

This daylight exposure table for Kodak Verichrome Pan Film is similar to the ones you'll find in the film instruction sheets packaged with all other Kodak films. These are average settings. For back-lighted close-ups, give two full stops more exposure.

Negative grain and what causes it

Let's say that boredom or an irresistible compulsion has impelled someone to construct two recognizable pictures of the same simple object from two such highly unlikely materials as black ping-pong balls and black marbles. Observing both pictures from the same fairly close distance, you'd certainly be more conscious of and disturbed by the elements making up the ping-pong ball picture due to their greater size. Viewed from far off, however, the pictures would be likely to look identical.

In a very exaggerated way, this describes a variable characteristic of photographic films. To make one film emulsion more sensitive to light than another, you must use larger crystals of silver bromide. After development, the grains of black silver formed from these crystals will also be larger than those in less light-sensitive films.

This difference isn't even faintly noticeable in prints of the size produced by commercial photofinishers. It generally isn't apparent either in moderate-size enlargements, up to about seven or eight times the dimensions of the original negative. When the degree of enlargement is really considerable, though, the prints made from extremely light-sensitive films, such as Kodak Tri-X, will show what looks like a salt-and-pepper effect in the gray, middle-tone areas. This is called graininess. The fine-grain films, such as Kodak Panatomic-X, are not entirely grain-free but will abide a much greater degree of enlargement before the graininess becomes apparent.

In a way, graininess is the price a picture taker often must pay for the advantage of a very light-sensitive film.

Color sensitivity of black-and-white films

The range of color sensitivity in various photographic films not only spans the rainbow but actually surpasses it by edging into invisible ultraviolet and infrared radiation.

Many films manufactured for use in preparing printing plates respond only to blue illumination.

The sensitivity of infrared films includes not only the radiation that gives them their name, but red and blue as well. In most applications, this blue sensitivity serves no useful function and is purposefully eliminated by placing a red filter over the camera lens.

Until quite recently, the most common, all-around snapshot films were orthochromatic, that is, responsive to blue and green light but blind to red. This tended to produce pictures in which lips and other facial features were unnaturally dark and blue skies turned out extremely pale.

Except in some specialized adaptations where this sort of sensitivity is advantageous (portraiture of men is one), ortho films have largely been replaced by panchromatic materials. "Pan" sensitivity takes in all visible colors and makes the most natural, representative pictures. All current Kodak black-and-white roll films are panchromatic.

Lenses and lens markings

But for one disqualifying shortcoming, a disk of glass cut from the finest-quality milk bottle might be an entirely satisfactory resident of a camera's front porthole. It simply cannot focus. The most prominent characteristic that separates a lens from all other manner of glassware is its ability to project a sharp, distinct image.

After all, as film lies in a darkened camera, it is little more than a flat, image-retaining screen. To acquire any utility, it must have projected upon it some sort of picture. For the film to reproduce the picture recognizably, the picture should reach it as millions of tiny pinpoints of light. This is precisely what an accurately-focused lens does. If the lens isn't accurately focused, or if it is incorrectly shaped, it will tend to project only blobs of light, rather than pinpoints, and create an indistinct, unsharp image.

Another vital requisite of a good lens is that it focus equally well across the entire area of the film. All lenses have rounded surfaces. Film is flat. These rounded glass optics should be designed so that they throw onto the film a picture that is as distinct and bright in the corners as in the center.

Ordinarily, there are two numbers engraved on a camera lens of the adjusting type. One is the focal length. It is measured in millimeters which convert to the English system at the rate of about twenty-five to the inch. Focal length is the distance from a certain point in the lens to the film when the lens has been focused on a faraway point. This is the ∞ or "infinity" marking on the camera focusing scale and as near as the lens ever approaches the film. To create size and depth relationships which pretty much match those transmitted by our eyes, lens focal length should about equal the diagonal of the camera's negative size. In nearly all still cameras, this is the case.

Some precision cameras have facilities for interchanging lenses of different focal length. A lens with a shorter focal length than the negative diagonal will include in the picture a greater area of the scene before the camera, but, by doing so, make all objects seem smaller and farther away. It tends to stretch distance relationships. One of longer focal length takes a narrower view of the scene and makes the objects in the picture seem closer and larger while, at the same time, compressing distance.

The other number on the lens is one preceded by f or f-. Briefly, f-numbers are measurements of a lens' light-transmitting power. Each lens has a maximum f-opening, just as each automobile engine has a maximum horsepower, although it's seldom necessary to call upon either. This

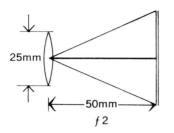

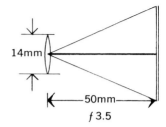

number is calculated through dividing the lens's focal length by its greatest effective diameter. If the focal length of a lens should be 50 mm (as it is on many 35mm cameras) and the maximum effective diameter is 25 mm, the lens is considered an f 2 lens. Should the maximum effective diameter be 14 mm, it would be an f 3.5 lens.

The closer the relationship between effective diameter and focal length, the greater the amount of light that will reach the film and the more useful the lens becomes for making pictures under dim illumination. One might expect, then, that all cameras would carry the very largest lenses that could be fitted to them.

Unfortunately, though, glass behaves in a highly uncooperative way. As you try to bring effective diameter closer and closer to focal length, you encounter ever-increasing difficulty in maintaining sharpness. A good f 11 lens can be made from a single piece of glass. As you design f 8 and f 5.6 and f 4 lenses, however, additional optical elements must be added to correct failings and preserve sharpness, so that most lenses in adjustable cameras are actually lens systems composed of several lens units.

Of course, a lens is seldom used at its maximum f-opening. Particularly in bright sunlight, it becomes essential to have a smaller opening. For this reason, the lens systems of adjustable cameras have a diaphragm which is capable of reducing the circular area of the lens through which light can enter. The action of this diaphragm can be observed by opening the back of the camera, looking into the lens and shifting from one f-number to another. Each f-number on the camera scale is computed by the same ratio, focal length to effective diameter, as the maximum f-number.

Lens opening or *f*-number, whichever term you choose, has a great deal of influence on the range of sharpness in your pictures. Every time you snap a picture with the lens focused at ten feet, everything exactly ten feet from the camera should turn out sharp because its image reaches the film as pinpoints of light. The objects closer or farther away reach the film as small circles of light either on the way to becoming pinpoints or spreading out again after having made them somewhere in front of the film plane. These are called "circles of confusion."

If the circles of confusion are extremely small, we can't distinguish them from the pinpoints. This makes the objects near the plane on which you've focused appear to be in perfect focus too. Objects much nearer or much farther away, since they reach the film as ever-increasing blobs of light, begin to look fuzzy.

When the lens's effective diameter is very large, the circles of confusion also tend to be quite large, even when close to the plane of focus. When the diameter is small, however, the circles are squeezed down and reduced in size. Since these smaller circles more nearly approach the size of the pinpoints, lens openings like *f* 11 and *f* 16 make it a great deal easier to achieve both near and far things in sharp focus.

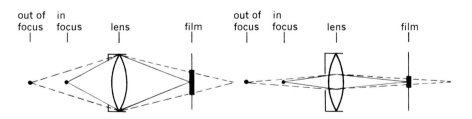

out of focus   in focus   lens   film   out of focus   in focus   lens   film

Everything at the distance for which the camera lens is focused reaches the film as pinpoints of light. Everything nearer or farther reaches it as relative blobs, but small lens openings squeeze these blobs down so they more nearly approximate pinpoints.

The old family album, modern style

Has there ever been a single family-situation comedy, either in print, on radio, on television, or in the movies, during which the young heroine's proud parents didn't positively mortify her by dragging out the old family album for perusal by her big heartthrob? This is no indictment of family albums as corny, old hat, or ludicrous. Actually, they are important documents. It's merely a warning that make-believe has no monopoly on this sort of occurrence and, as children grow older, you can hardly perform a more compassionate deed than by filing all nude-baby shots of the bearskin rug kind in some special, personal book so that the helpless subject thereof will never find them a source of embarrassment.

The family snapshot album is as typically, traditionally American as hot dogs and hominy grits. It is an institution, though, that has changed with the times and today is capable of achieving the documentary, modern look of photojournalism which, in a sense, it truly is. The successful picture magazines furnish an excellent model for a family album, not only in the kind of photographs they publish but also in the way these photographs are organized. Anyone can easily enhance the continuing interest of an album by following in their footsteps.

First, the snapshots taken of family members and family activities should be made so that they tell a story. The best, most memorable ones are worth enlarging. When you mount them in an album (gray pages are best for color snapshots), keep them in story-telling order. Then, caption them. There are few more fragile vessels than the human memory, and captioning will be invaluable in the future for recalling long-forgotten faces and dates. If you plan to type your captions, you'll find adhesive-backed, pressure-sensitive papers an ideal medium. They wind into a typewriter just as any ordinary paper does, and after typing them, you merely cut them into caption strips, remove the protective backing, and press them into their

JEFF'S FIRST HAIRCUT

started a bit hesitantly...

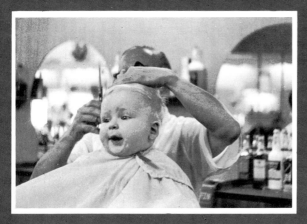

but he soon began enjoying the experience,..

even the electric clippers..

and a touch of bay rum.

proper positions. Many art-supply and stationery stores either carry or can obtain this material.

Many adhesives have ingredients which cause fading in photographic prints. Be sure the one you use in your album is safe for this application. Kodak Rapid Mounting Cement has been manufactured specifically to avoid this danger and is ideal for all-around gluing.

Photographic greeting cards

A more recent innovation for capitalizing on your best snapshots is through photographic greeting cards. There are few more truly appreciative ways of saying "Thank you" for a wedding gift than combining the thought with a snapshot of the bride and groom.

By far their most widespread use comes at Christmas time. Nearly everyone has on his greeting list many, many people who, because of distance, are seen much less frequently than he'd like. A photographic card, by including a special personal touch, adds an extra measure of warmth to the seasonal wishes you extend these people. These cards are especially valued when there are children in your family, since the snapshot, as nothing else, keeps your friends closely in touch with the growing-up process.

All that's needed for a good photo greeting is a good negative. Simply take it to a Kodak dealer and leaf through his assortment of greeting-card designs. Make your choice, hand the negative over, and tell him the quantity you'd like. He'll take care of the rest, even to supplying envelopes.

Just one word of warning. Start early.

Ordering enlargements

A good, sharp negative will yield good enlargements. In ordering enlargements, you can often obtain better pictures than the original prints by cropping. This involves making your enlargement from less than the full negative area by cropping in from one or more sides. With four straightedges and two "L's," you can experiment on the print to see whether cropping is feasible and advantageous.

If it is, place some marks on the borders of the original print to show exactly what area you want the enlargement to include and give this to your dealer when placing the enlarging order.

Remember that prints can always be replaced if you still have the negative and if it is in good condition. Negatives, though, are virtually irreplaceable and should be carefully safeguarded. They can be safely kept either in special negative files sold in most camera shops, or in the envelopes returned to you by your dealer. The vital point, though, is that they be handled only by the edges and be kept in a fairly dry, temperate, dark location.

Any original snapshot may contain the elements of a good picture but also a great deal of extraneous material around the outer edges. Before ordering an enlargement, check with two "L's" or four straightedges on your print and find out whether using only part of the negative will give you a better enlargement. To see how this one was improved, turn to the next page.

This enlargement closes right in on the main action of the original negative and dispenses with all unimportant detail.

Showing off your slides

Color slides, of course, are made to be shown, even shown off. Unless they are shown well, however, they lose much of their effectiveness. If you plan to project some of your slides for the entertainment of a group, the best means of assuring that they *will* be entertaining is by taking a few minutes to organize them into some logical sequence. Cull thoroughly and ruthlessly so that you weed out the poor and repetitive ones that tend to bore even family audiences. Try to select pictures as interesting to others as they are to you. Just simple thoughtfulness like this will assure that your friends will look forward to your slide shows with anticipation rather than dread.

Photography is a deep well and no single bucket is capable of collecting more than an infinitesimal part of its content. Should your curiosity o'erleap the confines of this volume, here are some other Kodak publications that, in a sense, pick up the thread of certain subjects at about the point where *How To Make Good Pictures* drops it.

Flash Pictures: Explores the way in which flash lamps produce illumination and relates this information to practical picture-taking requirements. It includes many different methods of employing flash equipment, offers a section on the manipulation of multiple-flash setups, and concentrates special attention on electronic flash problems. 52 pp

Kodak Filters and Pola-Screens for Black-and-White Films: Explains, with the help of numerous illustrations, the theory of photographic filters and contains information on a more extensive group of filters than is mentioned in *How To Make Good Pictures.* Data sheets are included for the most commonly used filters. 52 pp

Basic Developing, Printing and Enlarging: Lists simple, inexpensive equipment for home photographic processing and then, in step-by-step terms, tells how to use it. Shows how developing and printing can be carried out under ordinary room light. 32 pp

These are only a few of the many books and booklets on photography sold by Kodak dealers. Send a post card addressed to Consumer Markets Division, Eastman Kodak Company, Rochester, N. Y. 14650, requesting *Kodak Book List 1—Basic Picture Taking.*

HOME MOVIES

Some men of persistent curiosity proved many years ago that a group of pictures taken at very brief intervals, when projected rapidly, give a startling illusion of motion. To this momentous discovery, we owe "The Birth of a Nation," "Abbott and Costello Meet the Werewolf," and the fact that you, with the greatest of ease, can compile a movie log of your family in full color.

The mechanical end of home-movie making can be remarkably uncomplex. On such equipment as one of the Brownie Movie Cameras, the lens is prefocused, the shutter action is pre-set, and the only adjustment necessary is one for lens opening. Outdoors, this is determined by the brightness of the sunlight; indoors, since most movie makers employ a light bar which holds two or four photoflood lamps and attaches to the camera, it depends on the distance from camera to subject. All of this data is included on a small card packed with each roll of film—a card, by the way, that slides directly into a holder on the side of the camera and is always available for consultation.

More costly movie cameras offer such features as slow-motion shutter settings, fully focusing lenses, and instant magazine loading of film. Even with cameras in the Brownie series, however, you can enjoy the added fun of telephoto and wide-angle lenses through inexpensive converters which attach to the regular lens mount.

Most home-movie enthusiasts use 8mm equipment, since cameras, projectors, and films are all more economical than 16mm. Unless there is much likelihood of projecting your pictures on screens larger than five feet in width, 8mm will probably prove fully satisfactory. Should you have any thought, though, of showing your films to large audiences on auditorium-size screens, 16mm is a must.

Any Kodak dealer can tell you a great deal more about home-movie equipment, and should you desire a volume with the same kind of approach to movies that this book has to stills, he'll supply *How To Make Good Movies*.

190

INDEX